# Knitting
## Colour, structure and design

# Knitting
## Colour, structure and design

Alison Ellen

THE CROWOOD PRESS

First published in 2011 by
The Crowood Press Ltd
Ramsbury, Marlborough
Wiltshire SN8 2HR

**www.crowood.com**

This impression 2012

**British Library Cataloguing-in-Publication Data**
A catalogue record for this book is available from the British Library.

ISBN 978 1 84797 284 2

Photographs by Colin Mills

Typeset by Kelly-Anne Levey
Printed and bound in India by Replika Press Pvt. Ltd.

# CONTENTS

# ACKNOWLEDGEMENTS

Going back in time, my textile training at Dartington and Farnham Colleges of Art and their philosophy of teaching material- and technique-led design still remain an important influence. Thanks go to students from my knitting workshops, where I have learnt at least as much as taught. To my knitters: thanks for their skill and patience over the years, their input and enthusiasm, and their willingness to try something new. Particular thanks to Christabel Hedges and Janet Hawkins for checking patterns and helping with instructions and mathematics. Appreciation and thanks to those who knitted pieces for this book and also advised on instructions: Joan Brown, Betty Dobson, Betty Cottle, Tina Fenwick Smith, Christabel Hedges, Angie Harris, Janet Hawkins, Margaret Maher, Margaret Malony, Kneale Palmer, Clare Sampson, Yvonne Tatters. Thanks to Colin Mills for the photos and his inspiration in ways of displaying the work. Last but not least, thanks to my family and to Dan for their enduring support.

# INTRODUCTION

Properly practised, knitting soothes the troubled spirit, and it doesn't hurt the untroubled spirit either. When I say properly practised, I mean executed in a relaxed manner, without anxiety, strain or tension, but with confidence, inventiveness, pleasure, and ultimate pride.

Elizabeth Zimmermann, *Knitting Without Tears* (1971)

This book will look at hand knitting as a way of constructing fabric and three-dimensional shapes in a creative way, rather than following the conventional knitting pattern formula of describing flat, patterned shapes to be joined together by sewing. One of the attractions of knitting by hand is the flexibility and scope of the technique to produce fabric made in any direction from any starting point.

Using knitting needles, it is possible to create almost any shape, either two- or three-dimensional. Knitting can make a fabric beginning from a straight edge, a centre point or a corner, and can create something flat, textured, distorted, patterned, rough or smooth. By increasing and decreasing the number of stitches it can become sculptural, with the freedom to shape as you go. If you knit 'in the round', using a set of double-ended needles or a circular needle, all these effects can be made in a tubular form, again shaping within the spiral, tubular construction. Developing the idea of free

*OPPOSITE PAGE: Knitting in entrelac and undulating textured stitches.*

*RIGHT: Samples of bobbles, stripes, zigzags, entrelac and slip stitches.*

*Pieces knitted with no seaming, using sets of double-ended needles when necessary.*
*All the techniques are listed in Chapters 2 and 6.*

◀ **Pointed cube shape**
i)   Mitred garter st square base.
ii)  Pick up sts all round, knit.
iii) Divide sts into 4, decreasing at
     corners to pointed top.

**Pod** ▶
i)   Sideways segments,
     short rows both ends.
ii)  Pick up around one
     end.
iii) Knit and increase
     in the round.
iv)  Cast off with wiggles
     (exaggerated picot).

▲ **Dancing shape**
i)    Short-row segments circle.
ii)   Pick up stitches and knit border.
iii)  Pick up centre and rib a tube.
iv)   I-cords.
v)    Decrease circle every round.
vi)   Frill.
vii)  Picot cast-off.

▲ **Blue cube**
i)   Mitred square.
ii)  Pick up round edges and purl
     in the round, twisted knit st
     at corners.
iii) Mitred square, working in sts
     at sides for seamless top.

▲ **White shape, 3 legs**
i)    Knit 3-sided shapes, decreasing to
      I-cords, then picking up sts from bases
      to attach together.
ii)   Pick up all round remaining sts and K2,
      P2 rib in the round.
iii)  Knit, increasing out, then purl ridges.
iv)   Decrease inwards to point.

shaping further, stitches can be picked up from any edge or surface, and off you go again in a different direction, with no sewn seams needed. There are limitless possibilities.

This book will also look at how to use different combinations of stitches to alter the knitted fabric: the drape and weight of it, how it hangs, how stretchy it is, how thick or thin, open or solid. It will encourage thinking of new ways of constructing 3D shapes for clothing, accessories, items for interiors, or simply exploring the possibilities for making larger, sculptural pieces, small intricate pieces, or perhaps knitted jewellery.

My approach is to let the technique and materials lead the way, to experiment and see what happens naturally, even if the results are unexpected. Taking familiar materials and methods in new directions only needs an open mind, so that things going 'wrong', or making 'mistakes', turn into positive ways forward. If the knitting wants to behave in a certain way, how can we use it to our advantage? If it wants to curl up at the edges, then let that be developed into something that can be used. If a planned combination of stitches doesn't lie flat, or comes out with one edge shorter than the other, this is a discovery that can be used creatively in a design and can then be planned and controlled. The only doubtful element in a knitting 'surprise' is whether it looks accidental or deliberate, a mistake or a statement made with conviction.

Although the world we live in now has become much freer in its approach and there are fewer rules where fashion, clothing and interior design are concerned, so that things that would once have been considered unfinished and raw, or badly made, or old and worn out, are now accepted as a style or 'look', this does not mean that designing is redundant. It is still the case that a design has to look right and to be carried out with confidence: a dropped stitch, an unravelled edge, asymmetric shaping – it all needs to look convincing and intended in order to work as a successful design.

Experimenting with knitting is not something many of us have time for; it is simpler to follow a knitting pattern. However, if you enjoy being creative, it is worth putting aside some time to play and see what happens. As well as time, this takes a fair amount of confidence and courage if you haven't tried it before, and you may need a push to get started. It might help to attend a knitting workshop, go on a course, or join a knitting group. In this way, ideas and skills are shared, you may learn new or more efficient techniques, and there is the excitement of seeing how work has progressed, and the benefit of trouble-shooting problems with others. The Internet has become a huge source of information for knitters, from websites to blogs, and with some excellent, clear, well-paced video instruction available on line (bearing in mind that it is not edited, so some

*Fair Isle patterns, short-row shaping and edgings.*

is not so excellent): you can get instruction and information on everything from how to begin to more complicated techniques or information on different traditions in knitting.

Instead of following someone else's knitting pattern, experimenting can lead to ideas that are 'the direct result of the method of production'. (This phrase was written by Peter Collingwood, weaver, who studied different constructive textiles techniques in great detail, and wrote about them in an inspiringly clear and demystifying way in *The Makers' Hand* (1987).) In other words, you learn what knitting will do best naturally, and then develop your own ideas with it.

This book will suggest some ways of playing and experimenting, and will illustrate how stitches work and how using different stitch combinations can alter knitted fabric. It will encourage knitting without seams; why knit with seams when it's not necessary? The knitting patterns included in this book can be knitted as written, or you can use them as a starting point for your own ideas, improvising or changing aspects to suit yourself.

# Knitting Instructions

Communicating knitting instructions can be confusing. Originally skills would have been passed on by word of mouth and by demonstration until patterns began to be written down. Now we have a mixture of written instructions using confusingly abbreviated words, with different terms and abbreviations coming from different English-speaking countries, and we also have charts. Charts, using squared paper with each square representing a stitch, are an obvious tool in conveying colour patterns, but what about textures, knits and purls, slip stitches, cables and all the rest? There is the added complication in that squared paper doesn't give an accurate interpretation of the knitted stitch, which is wider than it is tall (in basic stocking stitch, at least), but knitting graph paper has been designed to overcome this problem, and symbols developed to represent the different stitches, including cross-overs, cables, slip stitches, increases and decreases.

## Abbreviations

| | | | | |
|---|---|---|---|---|
| alt | alternate | | oz | ounce(s) |
| B | back | | P | purl |
| beg | beginning | | P1B | purl 1 through back of stitch |
| bet | between | | p2sso | pass 2 slip sts over |
| cm | centimetre(s) | | patt | pattern |
| col | colour | | pss | purl slip st |
| cont | continue | | psso | pass slip stitch over |
| dec | decrease | | p-wise | purlwise |
| F | front | | rep | repeat |
| g | gram(s) | | RH | right hand |
| garter st | garter stitch: knit every row | | S | slip |
| in | inch(es) | | Sl1b | slip 1 to back |
| inc | increase | | Sl1f | slip 1 to front |
| K | knit | | ssk | slip, slip, knit |
| K1b | Knit 1 through back of stitch | | st(s) | stitch(es) |
| K2 tog | knit 2 stitches together | | stocking st | stocking stitch: knit 1 row, purl 1 row |
| kss | knit slip st | | tbl | through back of loop |
| kssb | knit slip stitch through back of loop | | tog | together |
| LH | left hand | | yab | yarn at back |
| M1 | make 1 | | yaf | yarn at front |
| mm | millimetre(s) | | yb | yarn back |
| no | number | | yf | yarn forward |
| O, or yo | yarn over needle | | yo | yarn over |

To my way of thinking, a chart is a visual representation of the knitted fabric. The symbols clearly represent the different stitches and looking at a chart gives an immediate impression of the surface texture. This is a clearer introduction to the knitting pattern than a page of abbreviated words, and a more intelligible one, giving immediate visual access to the finished item, and inviting an intelligent reaction and a creative response; it is almost as good as a visual image of the finished fabric, making it possible to imagine altering and personalising the pattern as well as simply following it.

If charts and symbols were to be accepted as universal, it would also do away with the words, making patterns comprehensible internationally. As this stage has not arrived universally, this book uses both charts and words, in the hope that people will be able to approach the patterns creatively and make their own designs from the ideas illustrated.

## Using Charts

The charts represent looking at the knitted fabric from the front, so the right-hand edge is where you begin the right-side rows, following the chart in the same direction as you are knitting, beginning at the bottom and finishing at the top. The symbols on the right-side rows are bold, and those on the wrong-side rows (which read from the left edge) are in plain, lighter print.

Each chart shows one repeat of the pattern, sometimes framed with heavier vertical lines. Any chart outside these lines shows edge stitches, not part of the pattern.

The symbols for knit and purl reflect the shape of the stitch as you look at it, with the knit being a vertical line, the simplest representation of how it appears on the front, and the purl as a horizontal bar. The charts show the right side of the knitting, so with the knit or purl symbol reflecting what it looks like on the front of the knitting; to reproduce a knit stitch on the front, you purl it on the wrong-side row. If you want to knit in the round following text instructions for knitting back and forth, there is a complication as you would need to make the opposite action on the wrong-side rows, reversing all the knits and purls in the instructions. If you use a chart, this problem does not arise;

*Stocking stitch.*

you can follow it for either back and forth or circular knitting. For example, we know that to make stocking stitch you need to knit and purl alternate rows when working back and forth, but the effect on the front is all knit, as shown by the vertical symbols

## Chart Symbols

|  |  |
|---|---|
| ❙ | knit on right side rows |
| ❘ | purl on wrong side rows |
| ▬ | purl on right side rows |
| — | knit on wrong side rows |
| ⟍ | knit 2 tog |
| ⟋ | slip 1, knit 1, psso |
| ⌐ | S2 purlwise, knit 1, pass both slipped sts over |
| ⋀ | decrease 3 into 1, see text for each method |
| ⊥ | slip 2 [by slipping the next 2 sts as if to knit them tog], K1, pass both slipped sts over |
| ●❙ | knit into front and back of st |
| O | yarn over, or yarn round needle |
| v | make 1 by picking up and knitting the bar before the next st |
| X | pick up the bar before the next st, put it back on the LH needle and knit through the back |
| S | slip 1, yarn at back |
| ⧖ | slip 1, yarn at front |
| ∼ | cable st left over right |
| ◡ | cable st right over left |
| ⌒ | cable 2 sts left over right |
| ℈ | knit 1 through back of st on right side rows or purl 1 through back of st on wrong side rows |

on the chart. If you knit stocking stitch in the round, you knit continuously (no purling) because the right side is always facing you – again, as shown on the chart. Charts make you aware of the effect of each stitch rather than blindly following words.

Where charts become a bit more complicated is when working a pattern where the number of stitches changes and the shape is not rectangular; then it is difficult to represent the shaping clearly. For the modular knitting patterns in this book, charts are used for the stitches only, not the shaping.

# CHAPTER 1

# KNITTING FROM PRE-HISTORY TO PRESENT

*Is knitting art or craft?*

Knitting is best called a craft. It serves life and is relatively ephemeral. It gets worn and wears out . . . It can be expensive, but is almost never precious … Therefore knitting is widely practised by non-professionals and tends to be a people's craft. Therein lies much of its interest and the fascination of knitting history.

Richard Rutt, *A History of Hand Knitting* (1987)

The history of knitting tells an incredible story. Studying it helps us to understand the technique more thoroughly and appreciate its potential in designing and moving forward. The different methods of producing a knitted fabric through time and in different parts of the world open our eyes and provoke questions. Looking at history also puts knitting in a social context and spotlights some extraordinary, as well as everyday, examples of skilled knitting.

## Earliest Examples of Knitting

Knitting is obviously a very old craft, but as is the case with all textiles, not much has survived the test of time for us to study. Most clothing and textiles were worn until worn out, often recycled or patched and worn out again, and of course fabric does not survive as well as other artefacts in hard materials such as pottery, metal or wood.

OPPOSITE: *Nineteenth- and twentieth-century cotton lace.*

The craft of hand knitting is thought to have begun in Egypt, where a pair of socks from the fifth century have survived. Whether these socks were made on knitting needles is doubtful. They are of a similar structure to knitting but the stitches are twisted: a technique that could also have been made with a sewing needle, working in rounds a stitch at a time into the row below, known as Nalbinding (*see* illustration in Chapter 2. There are other constructive textile techniques that look superficially like knitting but are different in structure, and again these are probably produced with needles of a different kind. Examples and diagrams of some of these knitting-like fabrics are shown in both Richard Rutt's *A History of Hand Knitting* (1987) and in Peter Collingwood's *The Maker's Hand* (1987), which has examples and diagrams of a huge range of different textile techniques. However the Egyptian socks were made, we can be sure that the technique was easily transportable, and did not need space or equipment to carry out. To weave cloth you need a loom, and although many primitive looms were portable, knitting, sewing, knotting, crochet and other techniques that needed no bulky equipment each had their uses for making different kinds of fabric and were therefore adaptable and ideally suited to a nomadic lifestyle.

## Tools and Methods

At some point, knitting began to be produced on knitting needles, and these too have been through various changes. Some early needles had hooked ends like today's crochet hook.

There are interesting links in styles of knitting and the tools used that indicate how the technique might have spread, such as the distinctive way of knitting with the yarn tensioned around the neck and manipulated with the left hand that is seen in Portugal and other European countries to the east and also some of the South American countries, suggesting that this method emigrated across the Pacific with the Spanish and Portuguese explorers. Hooked needles were used in these areas, and are still used now both for knitting and in the technique called 'Tunisian Crochet', where rows of knitting alternate with rows of crochet to produce a very firm fabric. Another obvious variation in style of knitting is whether the yarn is held in the right or left hand. This seems to have a regional bias. Although the UK has adopted a right-handed way of knitting, a large part of Europe and Scandinavia knit with yarn in the left hand, often described as the 'Continental' method. There are variations within these types of knitting, with many different names, often used in America where many different styles have come together. The differences lie in the way the yarn is held, and whether the main movement is in the fingers holding the yarn or the needles. The advantages of holding the yarn in each hand will be looked at in Chapter 3.

It seems that in many crafts a particular method of carrying out a process could become a habit over generations even if it was not the most efficient way of doing something. Was this because people had a different concept of time and were not actively searching for more proficient methods? Now we question everything and are constantly searching for more time-saving processes, but in the past skills were passed on in a natural and unquestioning way, sometimes resulting in techniques that seem labour-intensive and complicated rather than efficient.

*Knitted doll, probably from Central or South America.*

There seems to be general agreement that knitting spread from Egypt throughout Europe in the Middle Ages, with examples of sophisticated Egyptian patterned knitting in the eleventh and twelfth centuries, and fine two-colour silk knitting in Spain in the thirteenth century. Pattern using colour seems to have been produced in knitting earlier than the development of different textural patterns with use of knit and purl stitches.

Knitting reached Britain in about the fifteenth century, and travelled on through Eastern Europe, and north into Scandinavia. Trade routes took knitting in greater leaps to the Far East, and emigrants from Europe took it to the Americas and eventually to other colonies. Does this mean that men knitted? Certainly they did. Its portability made it ideal for carrying while walking: evidently shepherds in Spain and Portugal knitted, and probably sailors too.

## What was Knitted

To begin with, everyday undergarments, socks and hats or caps were knitted. Sock construction provides another example that makes a traceable link in the spread of knitting. There are several ways of shaping the heel of a sock, but there are examples of one noteworthy simple sock-shape still being

*Socks from Eastern Europe to the Himalayas, showing pointed heel shaping as well as short-row shaping.*

produced, described in *Mary Thomas's Knitting Book* of the 1930s as the 'peasant sock', that is similar in several countries, particularly in Greece and throughout Eastern Europe and as far as the Himalayas.

This sock is knitted as a tube from either the toe up or the top down, but instead of knitting the heel when you get to it by working short rows, half the stitches are put on a stitch holder for the heel, new stitches cast on leaving a slit, and the rest of the foot knitted, decreasing on each side to a pointed toe. The heel stitches are then picked up from both sides of the slit and, working in the round, another decreased pointed shape is made for the heel, the same as the toe shaping. This unlikely design works primarily because you can rely on the stretchiness of knitted fabric to adjust to the internal shape it is housing. Examples I have of this type of sock (which is still

made) are mostly knitted in a two-colour or 'Fair Isle' type of patterning which restricts the stretch, so they are not as fitted or comfortable as socks in a single yarn with contemporary turned heels, and there is more strain on the sides of the heel-shape than on a turned heel, but they work well enough to have been used over many centuries.

It must have been a huge step forward to have knitted stockings when before that time leg coverings were of woven cloth, needing to be 'cross gartered' or something similar to hold them up. The stretchiness of knitting is ideal for socks and stockings, and was the first indication of how beautifully knitted fabric works on the human body, moving and stretching with it, although it took several hundred years to cover the rest of the body and be developed as the 'jersey fabric' we know and love for so much clothing today.

## Knitted Underwear

Knitted woollen undergarments must have been immensely warm, and essential in northern climates in winter. Recent examples exist in museums: for instance, there are plain woollen petticoats in museums in Norway, knitted with fullness to provide welcome heat-trapping layers under skirts, and the famous 'Everest vest' in Shetland, Scotland, which became a popular export after the 1953 Everest expedition when one was made for Sir Edmund Hillary. Many knitted undergarments were decorative as well as functional, even if they were not on view. In the collection at the Victoria and Albert Museum, London, there is a Dutch petticoat knitted in fine white wool with ornate patterns of birds, animals and foliage, all in knit and purl patterning: an intricate piece of work needing hours of planning. Also in the same collection is a 'vest' from the time of King Charles I in fine silk, with both textured and coloured patterns, a knit and purl chequerboard edging, and gold thread used to make jacquard patterns. This vest is knitted in a simple T-shape with sleeves, but according to Richard Rutt, it may have been made on a knitting 'frame' (a primitive type of knitting machine) rather than on knitting needles.

## Knitted Outerwear

It was only in the late nineteenth century that knitted garments began to appear as outerwear in Europe, with 'the Spencer' and 'the Polka' (both fitted jackets for women) becoming popular. By this time knitting machines were developing fast, but alongside this industrialisation there were cottage industries that produced knitted socks and stockings throughout the nineteenth and into the twentieth centuries involving men, women and children; and as in other industries there was conflict between the two methods of production. With this parting of the ways, reasons for hand knitting began to change; it may still have been practical to knit by hand for wages in rural areas where it could be fitted in around other work, but it was also ideal for making one's own clothes at home with no need for extra space or equipment. By the beginning of the twentieth century, knitted garments were worn as outer garments for different purposes in different strands of society.

For labourers and working men, one type of functional knitted garment belonged to the community of fishermen living around the coast of Britain, and a tradition grew up of firmly knitted jumpers known as 'guernseys' or 'gansas', made without seams in a simple T-shape: a tube for the body, two

*Shetland women carrying kishies and knitting. (Shetland Museum and Archives)*

tubes for sleeves, and extra gussets under the arms and at the neck to give more freedom of movement. The evolution of this shape can be traced from King Charles I's shirt. They were knitted in wool, with patterns in purl stitches on a knit ground, and in some regions with cabling as well, the patterns evolving individually in different families and hardly changing over many years. Fishermen's wives could knit while they waited for the fish to be brought in; they could knit as they walked. There are early photographs of women in northern Britain knitting while carrying baskets of peat on their backs, so no time was wasted. Knitting was portable, sociable and an accepted part of this way of life.

The Scottish islands had developed coloured patterns in knitting, with beautiful examples of early pieces existing now in museums, while the tradition still continues. Often only two colours were used per row, but many colours were used throughout the garments in mostly small, repetitive geometric patterns.

A big change of direction came when traditional knitting was brought into high fashion by Edward, Prince of Wales, who had his portrait painted wearing a colourful Fair Isle sweater in the 1920s. The fame this brought to Scottish knitting did not affect the design of the garments, which continued to follow the traditional patterns, but it brought colourful knitting into acceptance as fashionable leisurewear.

*Gloves in traditional patterns from Shetland, Estonia, Russia and a hat from Peru, all in 'Fair Isle' technique with two or three colours per row.*

## Knitting Books, Patterns and Trends

As well as a wealth of knitted garments still existing now from these more recent times, our other sources of information are knitting patterns and books, which not only illustrate the styles that were popular, but tell us a lot about how knitting was perceived, who knitted and something about life at the time.

The earliest books had knitting 'recipes' with line drawings or etchings as illustrations, and it is amazing to us now to see how finely people worked: knitting needles as small as size 17 and 18 (today's equivalent would be 1.5mm or 1.25mm/ US size 000 and 4/0) were used with fine silk for socks and ties. If this is put into the context of other needlework such as lacemaking, embroidery and sewing of the time, it was not unusual – just breathtaking for us now to see how finely it is possible to work when our present world is geared to instant access, must-have and quick results, and it is hard to

imagine the hours spent on such detailed work. Early knitting books that are still around have a gentility about them, with illustrations of dainty hands holding the needles in rather refined manner; presumably these were for literate ladies knitting at home, whereas country folk passed their patterns on by example rather than following written instructions, so extending the tradition rather than looking to fashion.

Although there is a mass of opinion and information on the Internet, it is still quite easy to find period knitting books and research history at first hand. Here are a few books worth looking out for, written by people who have made a real difference to our knowledge of knitting and to the way knitting has developed socially, and who have also contributed significantly to pushing the technique forward.

Looking at books written in the 1930s and 1940s, a knitter who contributed enormously to the understanding and use of knitting was Mary Thomas, who wrote clearly and

*Knitting books on traditions, history and technique.*

systematically about knitting technique in two books: *Mary Thomas's Knitting Book* (1938) and *Mary Thomas's Book of Knitting Patterns* (1943). She designed her chapters logically, step by step through from the simplest stitches to the more ornate. As well as a few grainy photographs, her books are illustrated with plenty of very clear diagrams, but also with strangely quirky, humorous drawings, which as well as adding to the enjoyment and spirit of the books, make points which clarify how a stitch works and how it can be used creatively. At this time there was a limited choice of commercial yarns for knitting, and hardly any fancy yarns, so there was much more emphasis on stitches and technique to create pattern and interest. Mary Thomas's books do not give patterns but explain how stitches work.

Knitting patterns in other books from the early part of the twentieth century show a growing interest in fashion, and use stitches to create pattern and interest much more than later in the century when a wider range of yarns was available. Several of the more interesting early twentieth-century

patterns have been collected together recently in books by Jane Waller and Susan Crawford with advice on using them with contemporary yarns (see *Knitting Fashions of the 1940s* (2006) by Jane Waller, and *A Stitch in Time: Vintage Knitting and Crochet Patterns 1920–1949*, Vol. 1 (2008) by Jane Waller and Susan Crawford, which is a republication of the 1972 classic *A Stitch In Time* by Jane Waller).

Also writing about knitting in the first part of the twentieth century, Gladys Thompson's interest came from a different perspective to that of Mary Thomas. She did not discuss technique in detail, but recorded a small piece of knitting history by writing a book about the traditional knitted jerseys and guernseys produced in the fishing communities around the British coast in the early part of the twentieth century (as mentioned above). Here, the illustrations of the patterns that can be achieved with different knit and purl combinations are inspiring. Without changing colour, rich textured patterns are possible, firmly knitted in strong, smooth wool which shows up the contrast clearly between smooth stocking stitch, rough

*Early twentieth century cotton lace edgings, often made to edge household linen.*

purl, rope-like cables and gravelly moss stitch, all used to make thick, weatherproof garments with extra warmth over the chest and back to protect men working at sea.

Early books were not only instructional with basic 'how to knit' diagrams, but also increasingly contained patterns for garments ranging from the utilitarian such as underwear, bathing suits, socks and stockings, to smart classics. The authors were not always named as designers are today; many of the publications came from yarn companies such as Jaeger, Sirdar or Patons (later Patons and Baldwins). They were not aiming to design anything startling, remarkable or individual, but were more like the Marks & Spencer of the knitting world, producing patterns so that anyone could knit everyday clothes to suit all occasions, including some that are such classics that they could be successfully adapted years later to fit almost any fashion. The use of stitches to create interest was a vital element in the designs, and they were usually shaped with increases and decreases to mimic tailoring and darts in dressmaking.

## Attitudes to Knitting

After the Second World War it was still a cheaper option to make your own clothes, but eventually the time came when this was no longer the case (in dressmaking as well as knitting); and it became more economic and smarter (in the sense of dressing fashionably) to buy ready-made clothes. Perhaps it was at this point that knitting began to fall into low esteem, being perceived as frumpy. This attitude has continued for a long time, especially in Britain: hand-knitted clothing came to be considered dull, shapeless and amateur. The action of knitting was something for people who had nothing better to do, and for older women who weren't capable of getting out and about. It has taken an extraordinary long time for this attitude to shift. It still exists in Britain and can be heard still in the twenty-first century in the media, in jokes and in disparaging remarks about knitting, even though so much has changed over the turn of the millennium, with the USA leading the way for new excitement in knitting.

It is extraordinary that knitting is still regarded by some people as such a lowly craft when the start of the new movement in knitting that has propelled it from drabness to a medium for highly respected art and design began in the late twentieth century. The change can be traced back to the 1970s when fashion designers were beginning to make their names in knitting by showing knitted garments in their collections, and producing books of contemporary fashionable knitting patterns. These usually concentrated on using colour in new and exciting ways: the beginning of a completely different approach to knitting, moving away from the traditional and the classic to a sudden injection of strong statements from modern designers. Although knitting patterns had of course kept in line with fashion, bringing in the appropriate style such as the tailored look, the big shoulders, blouson jackets and so on through the early part of the twentieth century, now the 'hand-knitted look' moved to the forefront, becoming fashionable in itself.

## Designers

Whereas in the 1950s and 60s women would have carried their knitting with them at all times, knitting on public transport, at the cinema and at coffee with friends, by the 1970s its popularity had waned and young people were no longer learning the skills. Knitting began to represent old age and had become dull and boring, but at the same time new 'designer knitwear' became desirable.

Throughout the 1970s and 1980s there were different ways of marketing hand knitting, and 'designer knitwear' was available for sale at top-of-the-range prices. Finished garments were being sold both in the fashion industry and in the mushrooming world of craft fairs, but there was also a growing market for people who wanted to knit their own, in the form of kits and books. These fell into a bit of a vacuum, as the doldrums in knitting meant that there had been a slow decline in teaching children to knit and in the passing-on of knitting skills over three generations (more evident in southern Britain than in the north, Scotland and Ireland). An interest in knitting as an activity began to be rekindled, especially as this category of 'designer' garments were very much cheaper to knit yourself than to buy ready-made. Gradually more opportunities arose for learning to knit through courses and knitting groups and knitting began to spread again, with (thankfully) young people also catching the bug.

## Technical Books

Amongst all the books about knitting that have appeared over the past century, some stand out as major contributions to new thinking for designing, pushing things forward and sometimes sideways in a slightly different direction.

Taking a step back from the world of fashion, one knitter and writer who broke away from conventional knitting patterns and encouraged creativity was Elizabeth Zimmermann, writing several books in the 1970s and 1980s. These were not concerned with contemporary fashion and style but concentrated on investigating ways of using the technique creatively and finding different ways of constructing shapes, and have given birth to a whole new way of thinking. She managed to take an objective view of knitting (something that doesn't come easily if you have always followed knitting patterns), spending hours experimenting, questioning, wondering why things had been done in a certain way, and realizing that there might be a better way, or even a completely different way, and writing down her thought processes. Knitting did not have to start at the bottom and finish at the top, nor did each piece of a garment have to be made separately.

She will be remembered especially for designing the 'Surprise' jacket, which depended on the fabric being shaped within each row, turning corners by decreasing, so that the whole jacket was made in one piece (although not without seams) coming together unexpectedly at the end. This opened the door to thinking more about construction. Knitting can be built in any direction, and does not have to create rectangular shapes, but can change direction as it goes. This way of thinking had nothing to do with what was going on in the fashion world at the time; that was not her concern, but the fact that examples of her jacket design are still being made both for adults and babies, and can be seen in such a range of colouring, patterning and yarns, just goes to show how she stimulated individual interpretation, which was something new to emerge in the form of knitting patterns.

In a different way, and concentrating on technique, Montse Stanley also contributed a huge amount in writing books about hand knitting that clarify how knitted stitches work. She included such a range of different ways of achieving a particular effect that looking at her books is like having a new dictionary to help you understand a language more fully, making it possible to think more creatively. She was very concerned with detail and craftsmanship, pointing the way for good edges and finishes to each project; for instance, the subtle variations in each method of decreasing or increasing a stitch is covered in such detail, with such clear diagrams, that one can learn from her at every stage. It is also good to know that these techniques are preserved in her books. Her contribution also includes her large collection of knitting artefacts and patterns (now held at the University of Southampton), and her lecturing and TV programmes.

## Influences

The first person in the late twentieth century to make an impression in the fashion world was Patricia Roberts, who explored texture as much as colour, with cables and bobbles creating ornate and rich designs. These garments were high fashion and available to knit. They were also a challenge to knit, which was a big bonus for adventurous knitters looking for something new. Her shops and books had a huge following from the 1970s.

Kaffe Fassett's major contribution broke new ground with his use of colour. He opened people's eyes to using colour in a new way, with a freedom more like painting than following traditional knitting patterns, and gave us a kick-start away from convention and small patterns to a much freer approach. His books and his inspiring teaching made a huge impact, and suddenly anything was possible. The technique and its possibilities were not the main interest, but the use of colour and pattern were.

He came at the forefront of a wave of other designers who emerged at this point, influencing the way forward in colour and pattern through their work, their books and their teaching.

## Ways Forward

Leading into the twenty-first century, knitting has set off in yet another new direction. Provoked partly by the interest in recycling, there has been a boom in experimenting with different materials: fabric strips ('rags') will knit up successfully; paper and plastic in the form of recycled carrier bags; other materials such as string, raffia, recycled nylon tights – anything that can be manipulated on a pair of knitting needles has been knitted in the past few years.

The range in scale of knitted pieces has widened so that there is some incredibly small-scale knitting being produced, such as wire jewellery or as miniature knitted pieces, but it is also being made sculpturally on a large scale for installation and furniture, and also used in public places as political and social comment. With movements known as 'yarn bombing' and 'guerrilla knitting', reasons for knitting have also changed, leaving the original concept of making items to use and wear, and moving towards 'concepts' and 'statements', often called 'art'. Articles have been written about the social aspects of knitting, following the different ways in which knitting has been regarded and perceived in the last half century (Joanne Turney, *The Culture of Knitting* (2009)).

This brief summary or round-up of knitting trends to date attempts to put into perspective an overview of how knitting reflects and relates to our way of life. The next stage is to step back and take a fresh look at the technique of hand knitting, to explore how much more potential there is to be creative in knitting and to push ideas forward.

*Knitting in recycled materials including cotton fabric and plastic carrier bags.*

# CHAPTER 2

# STITCHES AND HOW THEY WORK

When you design [your own pattern], all these problems disappear. You knit to your own tension, your garments are made-to-measure and their style is exactly as you wish.

Montse Stanley, *Knitting, Your Own Designs for a Perfect Fit* (1982)

Examining something very familiar as if seeing it for the first time can be amazingly revealing and refreshing. Knitting and knitting patterns have been so much a part of our lives, it is easy to forget that this is a technique for experimenting as well as for following a given design. In fact, following knitting instructions can have a positively stifling effect on creativity, as often you are working blind without understanding how it all comes together until the end, especially if there are no clear diagrams. Although it's still exciting and rewarding and remarkably satisfying to follow a pattern, you are not always in control and the ability to think goes out of the window.

Taking a look at how knitting works, how it is constructed and how different stitches alter the construction, and therefore the resulting knitted fabric, can open the mind to thinking more creatively. So although the following analysis may seem at first ridiculously basic, it may help if you imagine you are being described a constructive textile technique you have never seen before.

*OPPOSITE PAGE:*
*Fair Isle patterns, short-row shaping and intarsia entrelac, knitted in dyed and natural wool, and silk yarns.*

*RIGHT:*
*Fair Isle and slip-stitch patterns. Centre leaf-pattern sample is the reverse side of 'wiggly lines' shown later in this chapter.*

## What is Knitting?

The structure of knitting in its most basic form is made in rows of loops, and as the rows build, the loops (or stitches) form vertical columns. This looped structure results in a fabric with stretch, making it dramatically different from a woven fabric where the threads travel in more or less straight lines vertically and horizontally.

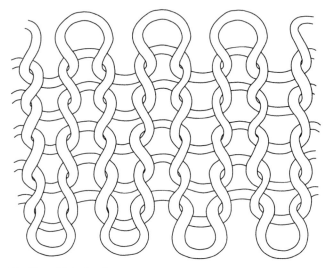

*Stocking stitch structure.*

There are a few techniques built in a similar way to knitting: one is Nalbinding (*see also* Chapter 1), which can look very like a knitted fabric with a twisted stitch, but it is formed with a needle and thread rather than the action of knitting on needles.

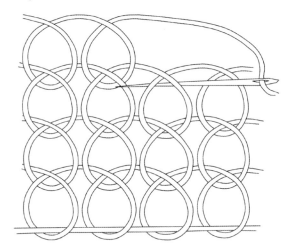

*Nalbinding', a similar structure to knitting but worked with needle and thread the other way up, forming twisted stitches.*

Another textile construction technique similar to knitting is crochet, with the fabric again built by looping the yarn, but in this case the loops pass over their neighbouring loops (in the same way as 'casting off' at the end of a piece of knitting), which makes a strong fabric and locks the stitches and prevents them unravelling, but also restricts their ability to stretch.

*A row of crochet, showing the way the loops link over each other like a cast-off knitted edge.*

## What Can You Do with Knitting?

These are some of the things that are possible when knitting by hand:

- Knitting a three-dimensional shape without sewn seams by picking up stitches and knitting in different directions.
- Changing the fabric radically by using different combinations of knit and purl, altering the shape without the use of increasing and decreasing.
- Constructing garment shapes that work well on different body shapes, that feel good to wear and will last well.
- Creating different fabrics for different purposes, whether open and lacy, for instance for clothing or for screening a window, or solid, thick and insulating for either clothing or furnishing.
- Using materials other than conventional yarn, knitting can be explored further with use of wire, fishing line, rag and so on.
- Knitting can produce colour patterning, ranging from using different colours for small repeating patterns, to textures built of dots (stitches) of different colours, or to broad sweeping designs with colours changing over different areas.

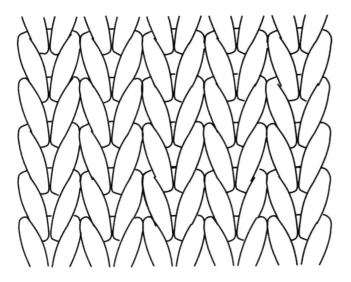

*Stocking stitch, knit side.*

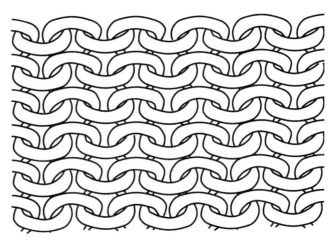

*Stocking stitch, purl side.*

## Basic Stitches

In its plainest form knitted fabric is made with all the loops passing to the back of the fabric, which is usually thought of as the 'wrong' side. When a stitch is made, it can be either 'knit' or 'purl'. Starting with a row of continuous loops or stitches on one knitting needle, 'knit' means making the new stitch by putting the second knitting needle through the front of the 'old' stitch and dropping the new stitch to the back of the first needle: 'purl' does the reverse, inserting the needle from the back and dropping the knitted stitch to the front.

So if you are working back and forth on two needles to make a flat piece of knitting, alternating 'knit' and 'purl' rows will make this smooth-sided fabric, sending all the loops to the same side by alternately knitting and purling rows. If you are working in the round, constantly working in knit produces the same effect, as you are always travelling in the same direction, in a spiral, and all the loops therefore fall to the back. This stitch is usually called stocking stitch or stockinette: smooth on one side, rougher on the reverse. The stretch of this stocking stitch fabric works in all directions, but is much greater widthways as the loops can stretch out further sideways, but are more restricted vertically.

This very basic information is something we absorb unconsciously when learning to knit as children and following knitting patterns, but in order to knit creatively, it helps to understand and look objectively at the structure we are making so that we can alter and vary it to get the results we want.

Also, if you have a clear picture in your head of how each stitch is being made and where it is going, it is much easier to see when something goes wrong through miscounting or dropping a stitch. A dropped stitch can seem such a calamity, but if you can follow it down its own 'column' and understand whether the loops fall to the front or back, it is much easier to correct.

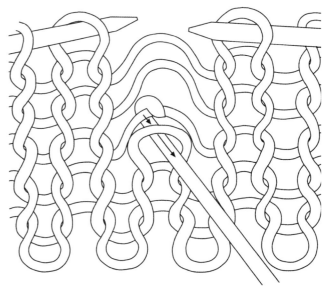

*Picking up a dropped stitch with a crochet hook.*

Stitch sampler, showing how stitches can alter the fabric. Each panel is knitted on the same size needle with the same number of stitches and rows.

From the bottom:

a) Garter stitch.

b) Stocking stitch.

c) Cable (made on a K4, P2 base, crossing 2 over 2 knit sts).

d) Moss stitch.

e) 'Twice knit' st:

**Row 1** K2 tog, only dropping the first st off the needle ,* K2 tog with the st remaining on the needle and the next st, rep from * to last st, ending K1.

**Row 2** Work in the same way in purl.

f) Purl-side stocking st.

g) Entrelac using a 6-st module.

*Stitch sampler charts*

*a) garter stitch*    *b) stocking stitch*    *c) cable*    *d) moss stitch*    *e) 'twice-knit' stitch*    *f) purl-face stocking stitch*    *g) stocking st entrlac*

The fun begins with the interplay of the knit and purl stitches. These two elements provide scope for enormous variation in design by using them in different combinations, but that is only the beginning: stitches can also be distorted and pulled in various ways, out of the bounds of their own row or column. They can be crossed over each other to make decorative twists and trellis patterns (cables), or to produce dense, strong fabric. Holes can be made (intentionally!) and used decoratively as in lace knitting. Stitches can be bunched together and pushed out again, and they can be increased and decreased within the fabric, making zigzags, ripples and bias fabric. We are used to the different patterns stitches can make on the front of the knitted fabric, and it is easy to forget or be unaware that these variations all affect the stretch or firmness, the thickness and the drape of the fabric as well as the look of it. Knitting can be thick and firm, thick and stretchy, fine and lacy, warm and cosy – without even using different yarns the scope for altering the fabric is enormous.

## Knit and purl

Stocking stitch fabric, although smooth, does not lie flat but has a natural inclination to curl. It curls away towards the purl side at the side edges, and inwards towards the knit side at top and bottom.

*Stocking stitch tends to curl at the edges, towards the knit side at top and bottom, and towards the purl side at the side edges.*

This tendency is noticeable in lots of stitches where knit and purl are combined. For instance, if alternate knit and purl facing stitches are worked vertically in columns as in ribbing, the knit stitch comes forward and the purl stitch sinks back. This happens when you rib K1, P1, or K2, P2, or any even or uneven number of each stitch; as long as the knits and purls stay in their vertical columns, knit always pushes forward, and purl sinks back. This does not happen if you change to a different yarn (or colour) for the different stitches, only when it is all worked in the same yarn, so it is the conflict that is set up in the change of direction from front to back that causes this to happen.

On the other hand, if you change from knit to purl horizontally, that is knit whole rows with the loops all falling to the back then change to purl with the loops falling to the front, the opposite happens: the purl stitches push forward and the knit stitches fall back. An example of this would be knit 2 rows, purl 2 rows, repeated. The prominent ridges are formed by the purl stitches, and the knits recede under them. Again, this may seem like stating the obvious, but if you are aware of what is happening, it can be used as a design tool and controlled. It is pointless to try to make the knitted fabric go against its natural behaviour, to expect something to lie flat when it wants to curl up, so it is more productive to go with it and see how you can use the structure to do what you want in a way that it is happy to do rather than to fight it.

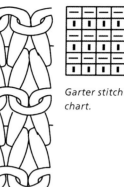

*Garter stitch chart.*

*Garter stitch.*

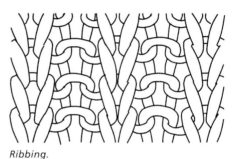

*Ribbing stitch chart.*

*Ribbing.*

*Moss stitch chart.*

*Moss stitch.*

*Welting chart.*

*Welting.*

Blocks of rib and welt squares.

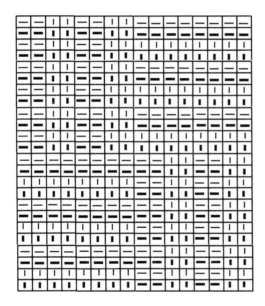

Rib-welt squares chart.

Three ways of making a flat edging:
Top: stocking stitch with a purl row 'ridge' to make a fold and stitch a hem.
Middle: garter stitch edge.
Bottom: moss stitch edge.

There are other factors that influence how the structure behaves; for instance a soft, limp yarn will curl less than a strong, springy yarn, which takes the shape of the stitches more energetically, and holds the shape more strongly (*see* Chapter 6).

If you don't want the fabric to curl at the edges, there are various solutions: it can be turned back on itself and hemmed into place so that the two curving surfaces counterbalance each other, or you can even use a different material to back it and to hold it firm. But then if you need to correct the way it sits, why knit it in the first place? It is more rewarding to find a stitch that will do what is needed naturally; there are many combinations of knit and purl that don't curl up and do make excellent edgings.

As well as influencing the way the fabric behaves, knit and purl stitches can be purely decorative, making textured patterns of knit stitches on a purl ground or vice versa. If the stitches are more spread out with variation in every row rather than in blocks or columns, they don't have the same influence on the curl of the fabric, but just stand out as individual dots and marks against a plain ground.

Sample shaped by rib and welting stitches pulling in and up.

Cast on 38 sts.

**Row 1** Knit.

**Row 2** Purl.

**Row 3** Knit.

**Row 4** Knit.

**Row 5** Purl.

**Row 6** Knit.

Keep the welting pattern going (knit, purl, knit: knit, purl, knit), but start introducing the ribs like this (the ribs begin in the centre):

**Row 1** K18, P2 (=centre), K18.

**Row 2** P18, K2 (=centre) P18.

**Row 3** As row 1.

**Row 4** K16, P2, K2, P2, K16.

**Row** 5 P16, K2, P2, K2, P16.

**Row 6** As row 4.

Continue in this way, in groups of 3 rows (knit, purl, knit), bringing in 2 more rib sts either side of the centre on the first row in each group of 3.

The band of ribbing will get wider and pull in the shape of the knitting.

**Row 7** K14, (P2, K2) twice, P2, K14.

**Row 8** P14, (K2, P2) twice, K2, P14.

**Row 9** As row 7.

**Row 10** K12, (P2, K2) 3 times, P2, K12.

**Row 11** P12, (K2, P2) 3 times, K2, P12.

**Row 12** As row 10.

**Row 13** K10, (P2, K2) 4 times, P2, K10.

**Row 14** P10, (K2, P2) 4 times, K2, P10.

**Row 15** As row 13.

**Row 16** K8, (P2, K2) 5 times, P2, K8.

**Row 17** P8, (K2, P2) 5 times, K2, P8.

**Row 18** As row 16.

**Row 19** K6, (P2, K2) 6 times, P2, K6.

**Row 20** P6, (K2, P2) 6 times, K2, P6.

**Row 21** As row 19.

**Row 22** K4, (P2, K2) to last 6 sts, P2, K4.

**Row 23** P4, (K2, P2) to last 6 sts, K2, P4.

**Row 24** As row 22.

**Row 25** (K2, P2) to last 2 sts, K2.

**Row 26** (P2, K2) to last 2 sts, P2.

**Row 27** As row 25.

*Rib-welt shape chart.*

Examples of these kinds of patterns can be seen in traditional fishermen's knits from the early twentieth century, examples of which are in museums or books, for example Gladys Thompson, *Guernsey and Jersey Patterns* (1955), Michael Pearson, *Traditional Knitting* (1984) and Rae Compton, *The Complete Book of Traditional Guernsey and Jersey Knitting* (1983). The patterns do two things: they look decorative, describing geometric zigzags, triangles, chequerboards and trellises or dot patterns, but this use of stitches also makes the fabric thicker and warmer.

## Cabling

Cabling refers to crossing stitches over each other, so they travel away from their vertical column, twisting with neighbouring stitch columns. This needs some extra manipulation: if only one stitch is to cross over another, they can be switched over on the left-hand needle before knitting, and knitted in the new order in the crossed position. If bigger groups are

*Purl stitches on a stocking stitch ground to make patterns, as used in traditional fishermen's guernseys.*

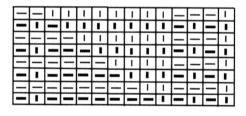

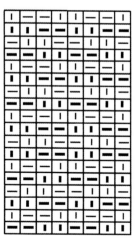

*Chart for guernsey stitches.*

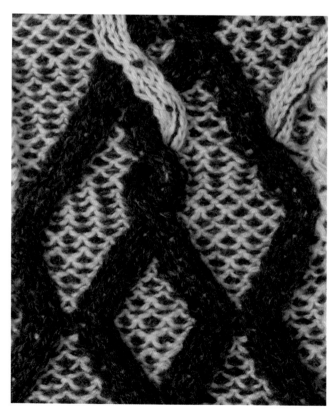

*Random cables, knitted in two colours, taking both yarns to the back for knit and weaving in the yarns, and both to the front for purl and weaving in on the purl side.*

## Ribbed cable

*Cast on 26 sts.*

**Row 1** (Right side) P2, * (K1b, P1, K1b, P2) * twice, P4; rep from * to * twice.

**Row 2** K2, * (P1b, K1, P1b, K2) * twice, K4; rep from * to * twice.

Rep these 2 rows until you reach row 11.

**Row 11** P2, * slip next 3 sts onto cable needle to front. Decrease next 2 purl sts by passing one over the other and knitting into back of this purl st, purl next knit st, knit into back of next purl st, purl next knit st.

Now work sts on cable needle: K1b, P1, K1b, P2, * P4; rep from * to * twice.

**Row 12** K2, * (P1b, K1, P1b, K1) * twice, K5; rep from * to * twice, knit last st.

**Row 13** P2, * K1b, P1, K1b, inc 1 by lifting bar before next st, purling it, P1, K1b, P1, K1b, P2, * P4; rep from * to *.

Now work rows 2 and 1 alternately again, until the next cable row. Make the cable row every 15 rows.

This pattern is taken from an Irish sweater in Gladys Thompson's book *Guernsey and Jersey Patterns* (1955), and involves increasing and decreasing as well as knitting (through the back) and purling during the cabling. This pinches in the stitches at the point of crossover, making it easier to cross the 3 stitches over 5 with a neater result. There is too much information to detail clearly in a chart.

crossing each other, a short 'cable needle' is essential to hold a group of stitches to the back or front while the next stitches are worked, then knitting the held stitches from the cable needle. The crossing motion pulls the knitted fabric in width-ways, making it thicker and narrower than a plain uncrossed piece of knitting. Cabling is usually carried out in a regular pattern of twists to look like rope: right over left, left over right, with lots of variations possible according to whether you knit the cables on a purl ground to make them stand out clearly, or vary the knits and purls within the cable.

However, there is nothing to stop the stitches travelling randomly across the fabric instead of repeatedly crossing over and back in the same way. It's tricky to make something random look intentional and to avoid distorting the fabric unevenly, but it provides an opportunity for a very free form of patterning that could be explored.

## Slip stitches

Slip stitches do the opposite to cabled stitches, pulling the fabric upwards and lengthways. In this case, instead of the stitches travelling sideways across their neighbours, they are pulled up across the neighbouring rows, simply by slip-ping the stitch from left-hand to right-hand needle without using the yarn, rather than making a new stitch by knit-ting it. Slipping stitches can make textured patterns that are slightly thicker and less stretchy than plain stocking or garter stitch: the stretch is limited both by the yarn being stranded behind (or in front of) the slipped stitches, and by the stitch being pulled up vertically across the rows. So there is another function here: as well as producing extra thickness, it holds its shape and prevents the fabric dropping. Slip stitches are particularly useful for knitting

## Criss-cross pattern

*Cast on a multiple of 14 sts + 2 edge sts.*

Always slip stitches purlwise, and carry the yarn on the wrong side.

**Row 1** Knit.

**Row 2** Purl.

**Row 3** (Right side) K1, S2 yab, * K10, S4 *; rep from * to *, ending K10, S2, K1.

**Row 4** K1, S2 yaf, * K10, S4 *; rep from * to *, ending K10, S2, K1.

**Rows 5 and 6** As rows 1 and 2.

**Row 7** K2, * S2 yab, K8, S2, K2 *; rep from * to * to end.

**Row 8** K2, * S2 yaf, K8, S2, K2 *; rep from * to * to end.

**Rows 9 and 10** As rows 1 and 2.

**Row 11** K3, * S2 yab, K6, S2, K4 *; rep from * to * ending S2, K3.

**Row 12** K3, * S2 yaf, K6, S2, K4 *; rep from * to * ending S2, K3.

**Rows 13 and 14** As rows 1 and 2.

**Row 15** K4, * S2 yab, K4, S2, K6 *; rep from * to * ending S2, K4.

**Row 16** K4, * S2 yaf, K4, S2, K6 *; rep from * to * ending S2, K4.

**Rows 17 and 18** As rows 1 and 2.

**Row 19** K5, * S2 yab, K2, S2, K8 *; rep from * to * ending K5.

**Row 20** K5, * S2 yaf, K2, S2, K8 *; rep from * to * ending K5.

**Rows 21 and 22** As 1 and 2.

**Row 23** K6, * S4 yab, K10 *; rep from * to * ending S4, K6.

**Row 24** K6, * S4 yaf, K10 *; rep from * to * ending S4, K6.

**Rows 25 and 26** As rows 1 and 2.

**Row 27** As row 19.

**Row 28** As row 20.

Cont in this way, shaping the diamonds by working the pattern backwards:

**Rows 31 and 32** As rows 15 and 16,

**Rows 35 and 36** As rows 11 and 12.

**Rows 39 and 40** As rows 7 and 8.

**Rows 43 and 44** As rows 3 and 4.

*Slip stitches can make large-scale, bold patterns, in plain-coloured textures as well as multicoloured patterns.*

*Criss-cross slip stitch chart.*

sideways or across a garment as the fabric has a tendency to drop or stretch this way, and a slip stitch will make a firmer, more stable fabric.

This technique can be used to create small textures but also free, large-scale patterning. There is huge satisfaction in using just one colour at a time but giving the illusion of complicated colour patterning by slipping the stitch across its neighbouring colour. The patterning depends on whether the yarn is stranded in front of or behind the slipped stitch; this is another device to be explored in pattern-making. It is worth getting hold of a good dictionary of knitting containing slip-stitch ideas as a short cut to seeing the possibilities.

## Increases and decreases

There are several ways of both increasing and decreasing to make different effects. Each method really does make a difference to the look of the fabric, and sometimes to its flexibility as well.

*Increasing*
- 'M1' means 'make one': there are four methods:
  (1) Knit into the front of the stitch, and before taking it off the needle, knit into the back of the same stitch, making a second stitch, then take it off. This makes a small mark in the knitting but no hole or gap. It can also be done in purl, or in a combination of knit and purl.
  (2) Pick up the strand or bar before the next stitch, and knit it as if it is a stitch; this leaves a small hole.
  (3) As above, but twist the strand before knitting it to close up the hole.
  (4) Pick up and knit the stitch from the row below before the next stitch, then knit the next stitch.
- Another form of increasing which makes a definite hole, used as much for decorative patterning as for creating extra stitches, is 'yo' or 'Yarn Over', sometimes written as simply 'O' for 'over'. In this case, the yarn is wrapped round the right-hand needle without inserting it into the stitch first (in the same direction as if you were making a stitch), leaving a strand of yarn over the needle that is knitted in the following row, leaving a hole.

## Slip stitch honeycomb

*Multiple of 8 sts + 4 extra.*

**Row 1** Knit.
**Row 2** Knit.
**Row 3** Purl.
**Row 4** Knit.
**Row 5** K1, * S2 yab, K6 *; rep from * to * ending S2, K1.
**Row 6** P1, * S2 yaf, P6 *; rep from * to * ending S2, P1.
**Row 7** As row 5.
**Row 8** As row 6.
**Rows 9–12** As rows 1–4.
**Row 13** K5, * S2 yab, K6 *; rep from * to * ending S2, K5.
**Row 14** P5, * S2 yaf, P6 *; rep from * to * ending S2, P5.
**Rows 15** As row 13.
**Row 16** As row 14.
**Rows 17–20** As rows 1–4.

*Honeycomb slip stitch chart.*

## Different methods of increasing and decreasing

*Cast on a multiple of 8 sts + 1 edge st.*

Purl 1 row.

Beginning at the bottom:

### Section A
**Row 1** K1, * M1 (make 1 by picking up and knitting the bar before the next st), K2, S2 (by slipping the next 2 sts as if to knit them tog), K1, pass both slipped sts over, K2, M1, K1 *; rep from * to * to end.

**Row 2** Purl.

These 2 rows form the pattern.

### Section B
Row 1) K1, * O [yarn over], K2, S1, K2 tog, psso, K2, O, K1 *; rep from * to * to end.

**Row 2** Purl.

These 2 rows form the pattern.

### Section C
**Row 1** * K into front and back of next st, K2, S2 (by slipping the next 2 sts as if to knit them tog), K1, pass both slipped sts over, K1, K into front and back of next st *; rep from * to * to last st, K1.

**Row 2** Purl.

These 2 rows form the pattern.

### Section D
**Row 1** K1, * pick up the bar before the next st, put it back on the LH needle and knit thro the back, K2, S2 (slip 2 sts one at a time), K1, lift both slipped sts tog and pass them over, K2, pick up the bar before the next st, put it back on the LH needle and knit thro the back, K1 *; rep from * to * to end.

**Row 2** Purl.

These 2 rows form the pattern.

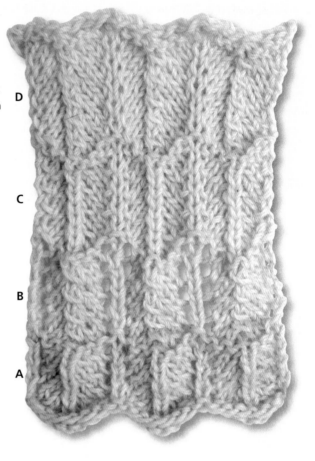

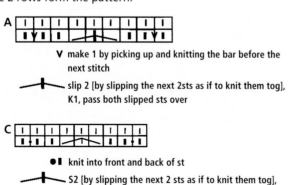

**V** make 1 by picking up and knitting the bar before the next stitch

slip 2 [by slipping the next 2sts as if to knit them tog], K1, pass both slipped sts over

●❘ knit into front and back of st

S2 [by slipping the next 2 sts as if to knit them tog], K1, pass both slipped sts over

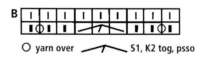

O yarn over ⟋⟍ S1, K2 tog, psso

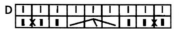

**X** pick up the bar before the next st, put it back on the LH needle and knit thro the back

s2 [slip 2 one at a time], K1, lift both slip sts tog and pass them over

## Decreasing

There are two methods of making two stitches into one: one places the left stitch over the right, and the other places the right stitch over the left. Again, this makes a significant difference to the look of the knitted fabric, for example in a raglan armhole where the decreases need to make a neat diagonal line mirroring each other.

- 'K2 tog' (knit 2 together). Place your right-hand needle into the second stitch together with the first stitch on the left-hand needle and knit through both as if they are one stitch. The left stitch appears on top.

- 'S1, K1, psso', meaning 'slip1, knit 1, pass slipped stitch over' (the knitted stitch). This is also written as 'ssk' or 'slip, slip, knit', which is managed differently but with the same result. Here you slip the next two stitches, pass them back again to the left-hand needle, turning them as you place them on the needle so you can knit them together with the right stitch on top. In fact there is a slight difference between the look of these two methods: in 'S1, K1, psso', the slipped stitch can become stretched and therefore not lie so neatly as in 'ssk'.

- In both cases the right stitch will fall over the left stitch, the opposite of what happens in 'K2 tog'. If you knit the two stitches together through the backs without the first part of 'ssk', that is turning them round, you will get a similar effect of right over left, but they will be twisted and therefore tighter, so will not match 'K2 tog' so well.

Both methods should produce perfect mirror-images of each other, and you need to know both so that when decreases form patterns, you can achieve a line that slopes continually in one direction, that is all to the left or all to the right. If you use the wrong decrease, you will get a broken pattern rather than a smooth line.

Increases and decreases are obviously ways of either creating more stitches, or of getting rid of stitches, and therefore altering the width of the knitting. However, they can also be used in pattern-making.

If increases and decreases are carried out at the edges of the knitted fabric, they will make it wider or narrower without distorting what is happening within the fabric. If they are made within the fabric itself, other things start to happen: the angle of the knitting is affected so that whole groups of stitches and areas will slope away from the extra stitches, or towards the decreased stitches. This is a fantastic design tool, inlfluencing the usually static columns of stitches to create curves.

## Trellis pattern

*Multiple of 14 sts + 4 edge sts.*

**Row 1** P1, K1b, P3, K2, (P4, K2) to last 5 sts, P3, K1b, P1.
**Row 2** K1, P1b, K3, Sl1f, P1, pss, (K4, Sl1f, P1, pss) to last 5 sts, K3, P1b, K1.
**Row 3** P1, K1b, P2, (S1b, K1b, pss, Sl 1 f, P1, kss, P2) to last 2 sts, K1b, P1.
**Row 4** K1, P1b, (K2, P1) to last 4 sts, K2, P1b, K1.
**Row 5** P1, K1b, P1, (Sl1b, K1, pss, P2, Sl1f, P1, kssb) to last 3 sts, P1, K1b, P1.
**Row 6** K1, P1b, K1, P1, (K4, Sl1f, P1, pss) to last 8 sts, K4, P1, K1, P1b, K1.
**Row 7** P1, K1b, P1, Sl1f, P1, kssb, (P2, Sl1b, K1b, pss, Sl1f, P1, kssb) to last 8 sts, P2, Sl1b, K1b, pss, P1, K1b, P1.
**Row 8** K1, P1b, (K2, P1) to last 4 sts, K2, P1b, K1.
**Row 9** P1, K1b, (P2, Sl1f, P1, kss, Sl1b, K1b, pss) to last 4 sts, P2, K1b, P1.
Repeat from row 2.

*Trellis pattern chart.*

## Wiggly lines, increases and decreases, reversing to leaf pattern

*Rep of 16 sts + 3 edge sts.*

This sample is knitted in 2 colours, one for the knit stitches, the other for the purl stitches, taking both yarns to the back for knit and weaving in (*see* Chapter 4) and both to the front for purling and weaving in.

**Row 1** * P3, K9, P3, K1 *; rep from * to * ending P3.

**Row 2** * K3, P1, K3, P9 *; rep from * to * ending K3.

**Row 3** * P3, K3, S2, K1, p2sso, K3, P3, M1, K1, M1 *; rep from * to * ending P3.

**Row 4** * K3, P3, K3, P7, *; rep from * to * ending K3.

**Row 5** * P3, K2, S2, K1, p2sso, K2, P3, K1, M1, K1, M1, K1 *; rep from * to * ending P3.

**Row 6** * K3, P5 *; rep from * to * ending K3.

**Row 7** * P3, K1, S2, K1, p2sso, K1, P3, K2, M1, K1, M1, K2 *; rep from * to * ending P3.

**Row 8** * K3, P7, K3, P3 *; rep from * to * ending K3.

**Row 9** * P3, S2, K1, p2sso, P3, K3, M1, K1, M1, K3 *; rep from * to * ending P3.

**Row 10** * K3, P9, K3, P1 *; rep from * to * ending K3.

**Row 11** * P3, M1, K1, M1, P3, K3, S2, K1, p2sso, K3 *; rep from * to * ending P3.

**Row 12** As row 8.

**Row 13** * P3, K1, M1, K1, M1, K1, P3, K2, S2, K1, p2sso, K2 *; rep from * to * ending P3.

**Row 14** As row 6.

**Row 15** * P3, K2, M1, K1, M1, K2, P3, K1, S2, K1, p2sso, K1 *; rep from * to * ending P3.

**Row 16** As row 4.

**Row 17** * P3, K3, M1, K1, M1, K3, P3, S2, K1, p2sso *; rep from * to * ending P3.

**Row 18** As row 2.

Begin again from row 3.

*Wiggly lines chart.*

Increasing and decreasing can be used to make columns of stitches bend and wave as they do in cabling, but in this case rather than crossing over other stitches, they are pushed and pulled sideways by the arrival or disappearance of stitches.

They can also be paired with an increase to move stitches around sideways without altering the overall number of stitches. This happens in a lot of lacy patterns: the increase 'yarn over' produces the lacy effect (*see* below), which makes a hole as well as an extra stitch, and either next to this 'yarn over', or a few

stitches away, a decrease will balance the number of stitches, and patterns are formed by the arrangement of the holes (*see below* for more on lace knitting). Increases and decreases can be used as a tool for producing flowing, natural curves.

All these types of stitches are being described individually to try to help you understand their potential. Of course they can be combined in all sorts of ways, but, like speaking a language, you need a basic vocabulary in order to speak, or in this case, design.

## Lace knitting

Increases and decreases are the basis of lace knitting. Patterns can be made with the 'yo' increase to produce holes. If you want to use the holes in patterns without increasing the number of stitches, each 'yo' needs to be paired with a decrease to keep the number constant. There is unlimited freedom in this kind of patterning; holes can be placed anywhere within the knitted fabric, in any grouping you want. There is a wealth of lace pattern instructions in books, including cotton lace mats, Shetland shawls and lace edgings – a fantastic eye-opener to skills developed over centuries in traditional ways, and plenty of inspiration for designing your own lace or holey patterning.

The decreases can help the structure of the pattern by leading the eye to left or right using the angle produced by the chosen method. If the decrease is always next to the increase or hole, the holes will dominate the pattern. If the decrease is a few stitches away from its paired increase, then all the stitches between the two will bend and slope away from the increase and towards the decrease. This can be developed to create movement in the fabric in the form of curves and swirls – a real bonus in a technique where you are bound by the grid of horizontal rows and vertical columns of stitches where it is difficult to create a flow, but if the stitches themselves are flowing and curving, the work is done for you. There are some wonderful traditional stitches such as 'falling leaf' and 'travelling vine' where patterns create vertical curves in this way.

*Lace patterns knitted in fine wool.*

In 'old shale' the curves travel horizontally; increases and decreases are used in groups within a row, and repeated again a few rows later, always above the previous ones. They do not move from their position in the row. In this way undulating waves are created by using several decreases alternated with several increases along the row, always ending with the same number of stitches.

## Zigzags

Zigzags are formed in a similar way, but this time with a sharp decrease (perhaps 3 stitches decreasing to 1), a few plain stitches, then a sharp increase (perhaps 3 stitches made from 1), followed by a few more plain stitches. Now instead of undulating waves, the stitches travel sharply up and down. The sample illustrated earlier in this chapter, shows several different ways of increasing and decreasing, each giving noticeably different results. The method of increase or decrease you choose really does make a huge difference to the look of the

### Old shale

*Cast on a number of stitches divisible by 12.*

A traditional lace pattern knitted in 4-row stripes. The 'O' (yarn over) makes a hole, giving an open, lacy look, but also allows flexibility so the fabric can move more easily than other kinds of increasing.

**Row 1** * K2 tog, K2 tog, (O, K1) 4 four times, O, K2 tog, K2 tog *; rep from * to * to end.
**Row 2** Purl.
**Row 3** Knit.
**Row 4** Purl.
The steepness of the wave pattern can be adjusted by the frequency of the shaping, so working 5, 7, or more rows before row 1 will make a more subtle, gentler wave. Repeating row 1 on alternate rows makes the wave steeper, but as the increases and decreases are so closely packed, it will also distort the fabric and make it difficult to keep flat.

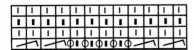

*Old shale chart.*

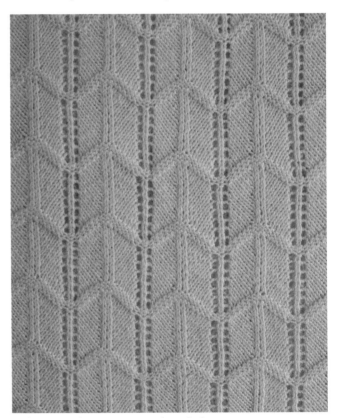

*Early twentieth-century cotton lace cloth.*

knitting. Different increases can make holes, larger or smaller, which give a lacy effect and enable the stitches to move about freely so that you might find you get a more exaggerated zigzag movement than if you use a more solid increase that seems to restrict the movement of the stitches more. Decreases have a very clear visual effect as well, because the stitch on top has a definite lean to the right or left; or in the case of decreasing three into one, you can also get a vertical line travelling up the centre of the decrease.

If you change colours in stripes in this kind of stitch, the movement is emphasized even more, revealing the zigzag structure. Something else is happening here as well; the stitches between the increases and decreases are travelling diagonally, leaning as described before from the increases where new stitches are created to the decreases where they are being swallowed up. What happens if the structure of the fabric is diagonal? You have a 'bias' fabric, and as in woven fabric, this has a completely different drape and stretch.

## Bias fabrics

Increases and decreases also play a big part in bias knitting. The knitting does not have to zigzag to be on the bias. You can increase at one side of your knitting and decrease the other edge, to make all the stitches travel across diagonally. If the knitting is increased at the right-hand edge and decreased at the left, the stitches will slope to the left. To make the fabric slope in the opposite direction, reverse the shaping. The whole fabric will slope, so if you hold your knitting to give vertical edges, you will find you get a sloping bottom and top edge; in other words you are making a rhomboid rather than a rectangle.

If you repeat increases and decreases along the row, always keeping them above one another, you are back to zigzags, but you can alter the number of stitches between for different effects, making each area of slope as big as you want. Single increases and decreases along the row will still result in the whole fabric sloping, whereas a double increase alternated with a double decrease (as described above for zigzags) will produce vertical edges and a zigzag top and bottom. Any number of patterns can be made in this way, and enhanced or emphasized with use of colour stripes or change of stitch in stripes to highlight this movement.

## Zig zag stripes

*Cast on a multiple of 17 sts, and work stripes, changing colours every 4 rows.*

In this sample, the decreases are paired in mirror image, and the increases, 'M1', are made by picking up the bar before the next stitch and knitting it. This does not leave such a big hole as 'yarn over' but still allows the stitches to move into the zigzag smoothly.

**Row 1** * K2 tog, K6, M1, K1, M1, K6, S1, K1, psso *; rep from * to *.
**Row 2** Purl.

*Zigzag stripes chart.*

## Bias zigzag stitch

*Cast on a multiple of 22 sts + 2 edge sts.*

In this sample, the increases and decreases are single, not paired, so the whole fabric slopes.
**Row 1** S1, K1, psso, * K9, M1, K11, S1, K1, psso *; rep from * to *.
**Row 2** Purl.

*Bias zigzag chart.*

## Modular knitting

Other stitches and ways of constructing knitting also result in bias fabric, such as 'modular' knitting, where the knitting is made in modules one at a time, rather than knitting all across the total width of the fabric. This term can mean any kind of knitting where each module is knitted individually and the stitches picked up from the previous module so it is all joined as it goes; but it is often used to describe just one of these methods, which is also called 'domino' or 'mitred' knitting.

Each module is shaped by decreasing, starting with any number of stitches and decreasing until all the stitches have gone, at one or more points within each row. The placing of the decreases can be either in the centre to give a mitred corner, or in several places to give several corners (to make an L-shape, for example), or with three or four decreases arranged within the row to curve the knitting into a scallop shape (*see* Pattern 7, Chapter 7). Many tessellated shapes can be knitted in this way, picking up the stitches from the neighbouring shape, so that they are all joined by knitting.

*Square module*
- If you want to use the modules as squares to make a flat base and sides, follow the diagram.
- Decide which decrease to use for the effect you want. Some decreases make a sharper point, whereas you could work with an even number of stitches and make two decreases, on either side of the centre, to make a less pointed edge.

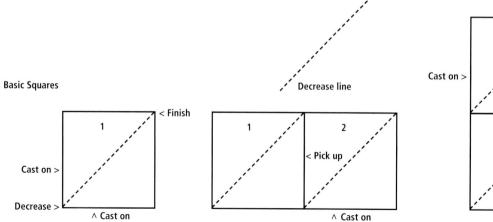

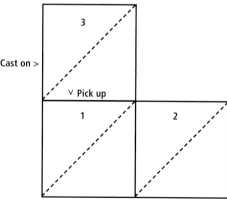

*Modular knitting, using the modules as squares.*

## Garter stitch

The way a module with a mitred decrease is made is to cast on an edge, and knit with a decrease in the middle of the row which travels straight to the finished point, so the knitting bends round at right angles and the cast-on edge becomes two sides of the finished module.

Garter stitch produces a flat square, as garter stitch pulls up lengthways. This structure uses twice as many rows as there are stitches to complete the shape, so in garter stitch, twice as many rows as stitches makes (more or less) a square.

**Garter st with stripe**
Cast on 41 sts, using a cast-on that is not tight, as this will stop the square lying flat. Use 'Knit-on cast on': make a st on LH needle, * knit into it to make next st, and put new st on LH needle. Rep from *. Don't knit between the stitches as this is too firm.
Knit 1 row.
Right side, begin pattern:
**Row 1** K19, S1, K2 tog, psso, K19.
**Rows 2 and 4** Knit.
**Row 3** K18, S1, K2 tog, psso, K18.
**Row 5** Change colour for stripe, K17, S1, K2 tog, psso, K17.
**Row 6** Purl.
**Row 7** Change back to original colour, K16, S1, K2 tog, psso, K16.
**Row 8 and all even rows** Knit.
**Row 9** K15, S1, K2 tog, psso, K15.
**Row 11** K14, S1, K2 tog, psso, K14.
**Row 13** K13, S1, K2 tog, psso, K13.
**Row 15** K12, S1, K2 tog, psso, K12.
**Row 17** K11, S1, K2 tog, psso, K11.
**Row 19** K10, S1, K2 tog, psso, K10.
**Row 21** K9, S1, K2 tog, psso, K9.
**Row 23** K8, S1, K2 tog, psso, K8.
**Row 25** K7, S1, K2 tog, psso, K7.
**Row 27** K6, S1, K2 tog, psso, K6.
**Row 29** K5, S1, K2 tog, psso, K 5.
**Row 31** K4, S1, K2 tog, psso, K4.
**Row 33** K3, S1, K2 tog, psso, K3.
**Row 35** K2, S1, K2 tog, psso, K2.
**Row 37** K1, S1, K2 tog, psso, K1.
**Row 39** S1, K2 tog, psso.
Break off yarn and pull thread through last stitch to fasten off.

## Double module

*See* Chapter 7, the end of Pattern 1 for making a rectangle or double square.

## Diamond module

If you want to use the modules as a 'diamond' shape with the decrease line travelling vertically, work enough individual diamond shapes for the base of your design, then make the next row by picking up stitches from two previous modules.

Place the two modules you are going to pick up from facing the way you want them, then pick up 15 stitches along the edge of one module starting at the right-hand end of your new base, pick up 1 stitch from tip of the diamond, pick up 15 stitches along edge of next module, and make as before. You could of course pick up from any edge, and make a design with the decreases facing in different directions.

This kind of knitting is often done in garter stitch, particularly the mitred square (or diamond, depending on which way you use it). Although there are twice as many rows as stitches in each module, garter stitch draws up the knitting to form the square shape and the finished piece will therefore lie flat.

*Garter stitch chart.*

## Stocking stitch

Using other stitches such as stocking stitch, welting and ribbing changes the proportions of the module, pulling up or in, in different ways, so that when these are fitted together, the fabric distorts: this is a great design tool for creating textured surfaces.

Cast on 41 sts as for the garter stitch sample, and work in the same way, knitting the right side rows and purling the wrong side rows to make stocking stitch.

This module is elongated with longer side edges than the cast on edge, and curls at the edges.

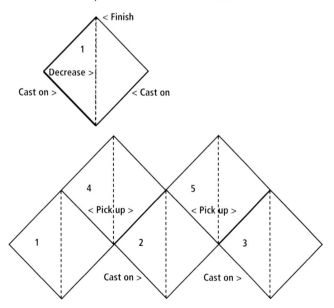

*Modular knitting, using the modules as diamond shapes.*

*Diamond shape in stocking stitch.*

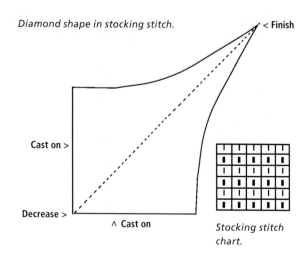

*Stocking stitch chart.*

## Welting stripes in 2 colours, A and B

Using col A, cast on 41 sts, knit 1 row.

**Row 1** (Right side) P19, S1, K2 tog, psso, P19.

**Row 2** Knit.

**Row 3** Using col B, K18, S1, K2 tog, psso, K18.

**Row 4** Purl.

**Row 5** Using col A, K17, S1, K2 tog, psso, P17.

**Row 6** Knit.

**Row 7** P17, S1, K2 tog, psso, P17.

**Row 8** Knit.

**Row 9** Using col B, K16, S1, K2 tog, psso, K16.

**Row 10** Purl.

Carry on in this way, decreasing on the centre 3 sts of every right-side row, in this 6-row pattern:

Using col A, knit, knit, purl, knit; using col B, knit, purl.

Finish off as in the garter stitch sample.

This module pulls up so that the cast-on edges of the patch are longer than the side edges.

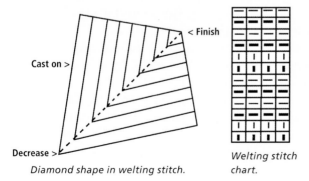

*Diamond shape in welting stitch.*

*Welting stitch chart.*

## Ribbing

*Cast on 41 sts.*

Next row) (Wrong side) P2, K2 for 20 sts, P1(centre stitch), K2, P2 to the end.

Pattern:

**Row 1** (K2, P2) for 16 sts, K2, P1, S2 (by putting right-hand needle into next 2 sts as if to knit them tog), K1, p2sso, P1, (K2, P2) to end, ending K2.

**Row 2 and all even rows** P2, K2 in ribbing but always purl the centre stitch.

Continue in this way, working in rib but making the decrease on the centre 3 sts on all right-side rows.

This particular decrease will give a straight line up the centre of the module: use a different decrease if you want a different effect.

This module pulls in so that the cast-on edges of the patch are very much shorter than the side edges.

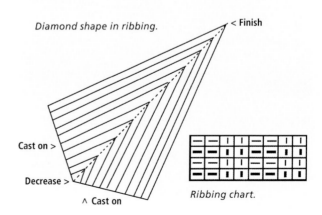

*Diamond shape in ribbing.*

*Ribbing chart.*

To sum up, the shape of the modules can be changed dramatically by using different stitches. The same construction in stocking stitch makes a diamond shape with two shorter sides and two longer sides, which buckles slightly when the pieces are joined as the longer sides have to fit with the neighbouring shorter sides. It is easy to experiment and results can be exciting and unpredictable. Think of the character of different stitches, whether they pull in or push out, and how they will react when joined in this way. (*See* Knitting Patterns, Chapter 7.)

## Entrelac

Entrelac is different again as there is no increasing and decreasing involved, but a stop–start change in the construction of each module that changes the direction of the knitting. The way that the construction in entrelac is different from mitred or domino knitting is that all the stitches for all the modules in the total width of the knitting are held on the needle all the time. The stitches are divided up into small groups or modules,

*Entrelac samples in ribbing (above) and welting (below).*

and one group is worked on at a time, backwards and forwards within its own group of stitches but joining with its neighbours as it goes. All the modules or blocks are rectangular and travel diagonally – the ultimate in 'bias' or diagonal knitting.

Don't be put off: this method is easier to knit than to put into words, which usually involve gesticulating as well to indicate directions, but the only option here is for words and diagrams.

### Description of structure

The bottom edge of each block is joined to a previous one by picking up the stitches along the side of this block, and the side edge is joined by knitting two stitches together at the end of its row. It can be made up of blocks as small as perhaps four stitches, or can be as big as you like. (I am using the word 'block' as each module is in fact a rectangle, having twice as many rows as stitches, so although often described as 'squares', they are much longer.) Any knitting stitch can be used in this type of structure, but we are used to seeing it in stocking stitch, which gives a slightly raised woven effect, as the length of each block makes it bulge up slightly. Different stitches such as garter stitch, moss stitch or welting will pull the rectangle back into a squarer shape, and it will lie flatter. Once you see how it works, it opens up huge possibilities in designing. The blocks do not have to be all the same size, as long as they fit together, so some blocks could be built of a group smaller ones that fit; for example four blocks of half the number of stitches of the large one would fit alongside the large one.

The most difficult part of learning entrelac is to knit a small sample with straight sides. It is an ideal stitch for knitting a circular garment, working in blocks around the tubular shape, first in one direction, then turning at the end of the round of blocks to come back the other way. If you are working in stocking stitch, you will be working in a round of knit-side blocks, then coming back with a round of purl-side blocks, and this is really straightforward.

However, to knit a shape with straight edges you need to start with triangles to form a straight base, and to make triangles at the beginning and end of each row of blocks to give straight side edges. Finally you need top triangles to give a straight top edge. Although at first this is complicated, once you have got your head round these different triangles, they are enormously useful tools in designing, as you can then make a straight edge wherever you want, for example at the front of a jacket, the bottom of a sleeve or to shape a neck.

# Basic entrelac, 6-st repeat

*Cast on a multiple of 6 sts
18 sts would be enough for a first sample).*

## (1) Base triangles

* P2 (this is wrong side facing), turn and K2, turn and P3, turn and K3, turn and P4, turn and K4, turn and P5, turn and K5, turn and P6.

Leave these sts, and repeat from * on the next group of 6. Work again, making 3 base triangles.

### First row of blocks (including side triangles)

NB colour can be changed for each row (or for each block).

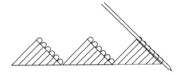

## (2) Side triangle

K2, turn and P2, turn; inc in 1st st (by knitting into front and back of st), S1, K1 (this is 1st st of next group), psso; turn and P3; turn, inc in 1st st, K1, S1, K1 psso; turn and P4; turn, inc in first st, K2, S1, K1 psso; turn and P5; turn, inc in 1st st, K3, S1, K1, psso. Edge triangle complete.

## (3) Knit blocks

* Pick up and knit 6 sts evenly along edge of next triangle, (turn and P6, turn and K5, S1, K1, psso) 6 times = 1 block complete.

Rep from * to edge of last triangle.

## (4) Last side triangle

Pick up and knit 6 sts evenly along edge of last base triangle, turn and P2 tog, P4; turn and K5; turn and P2 tog, P3; turn and K4; turn P2 tog, P2; turn and K3; turn and P2 tog, P1; turn and K2; turn and P2 tog. 1 st remains on RH needle, and edge triangle is complete.

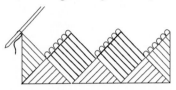

## (5) Purl blocks

Using st on RH needle, pick up and purl 5 sts evenly along edge of triangle just finished. (Turn and K6, turn and P5, P2 tog) 6 times, then cont as follows:

* Pick up and purl 6 sts evenly along side of next block, (turn and K6, turn and P5, P2 tog) 6 times; rep from * to end.

Knit blocks are now worked as before, but picking up from edges of purl blocks. Alternate the knit and purl blocks, with side triangles if necessary, finishing with knit blocks, then work:

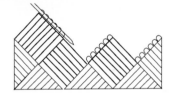

## (6) Top triangles

Using st left on RH needle, * pick up and purl 5 sts evenly along edge of block or triangle just worked. Turn and K6; turn and P2 tog, P3, P2 tog; turn and K5; turn and P2 tog, P2, P2 tog; turn and K4; turn and P2 tog, P1, P2 tog; turn and K3; turn and P2 tog twice; turn and K2; turn and P1, P2 tog, P1; turn and K3; turn and P3 tog; rep from * as many times as needed.

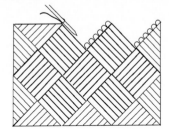

*Entrelac with different sized modules.*

*Short-row circle built from segments knitted sideways.*

## Short-row modules
## (circles, squares and darts)

Shapes can also be built using short-row segments; for example, a circle is easy to knit in short-row 'wedges', keeping the stitches on the needle, but leaving stitches behind and turning back on alternate rows so that only one edge grows. At the end of each wedge-shape the stitches are all still on the needle, so you knit all the way across and then begin again on the second wedge. The angle of each wedge can be changed by the number of stitches left behind: for example, leaving only one stitch at each turn means there will be more rows and a wider wedge. If you leave, say, four stitches each time, you will get a slimmer wedge, and need more of them to create a circle. If you use garter stitch, it will lie flat and grow slowly as it pulls up into a thicker fabric, but stocking stitch will grow more quickly.

Building circles in this way is a wonderfully simple way of making cushions, bags, spreads, shawls, or anything circular.

Try using it another way, and work each module or wedge in alternate directions, so that the longer edge alternates from side to side. This way a long strip can be made which has wavy edges and slanting rows: a great design tool, as stripes will accentuate the sloping structure, and depending on your chosen stitch, it can be reversible and used for scarves and other items where the reverse side will show.

It does not have to grow into a complete circle, but can make cone shapes using fewer modules, or if you go beyond the flat circle, it would make decorative frilled or flared circles and layers.

Short rows can also be used in shaping garments: either by inserting a wedge or 'gore' sideways into your knitting to spread out the shape of the body, (particularly useful in 'domino' knitting, see Pattern 3), or if the whole piece is knitted sideways, the short-row shaping can be used occasionally with areas of straight knitting between, so that, as before, one side will grow more quickly, but the straight rows ensure that the shorter edge will grow as well, to make the top edge of a skirt, for example.

Squares can also be built in a similar way from short rows, formed from four right-angled triangles. The cast-on edge becomes half the diagonal, and the outer edge is decreased, or the stitches can be kept on a holder to knit a border later. This gives the freedom to design a square cushion or spread with a different design in each quarter, joining them as you go.

## Small square made with four diagonal triangles

First triangle: cast on 12 sts for the base, which will form half the diagonal of the square.
NB if you want to graft this edge at the end to make it seamless, use a provisional cast-on: see Chapter 6.
This right-angled triangle is formed by decreasing at the edge that will be the outside of the square.
Knitting every row, decrease 1 st at the end of every right-side row, and continue until all sts are used up.
Next triangle: pick up the same no of sts that you cast on for first triangle, along the right-hand (right-angle) edge, and make second triangle (see small squares diagram below).
NB if you pick up your sts from the long edge, it will turn into a hexagon.
Make third and fourth triangles in same way, leaving one seam to be sewn or grafted at the end (see Chapter 6).

*Short-row insert to shape fabric (see Chapter 7, Pattern 3).*

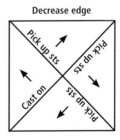

*Small squares diagram.*

## Circle knitted sideways, in segments

**Segment 1:**
Cast on 10 sts for the radius of the circle, and working in garter st:

\* **Row 1** Right side facing, K8, turn.

**Row 2** Knit back.

**Row 3** K6, turn.

**Row 4** Knit back.

**Row 5** K4, turn.

**Row 6** Knit back.

**Row 7** K2, turn.

**Row 8** Knit back.

**Segment 2:**
Knit all the sts again, turn and knit 1 row back and begin again from \*.

NB row 1 should always be right-side facing, with shorter edge on the left end of the row. Changing direction will make other shapes or an undulating strip: *see* Chapter 4.

Continue making segments until they meet and make a flat circle.

### Variations

This could be used to make a cone shape, or make short rows both ends of the row to form a sphere or pod: *see* picture in introduction.

Stocking stitch would grow faster but not lie so flat.

Each segment could be a different colour, or knitted in stripes to show up the direction of the rows.

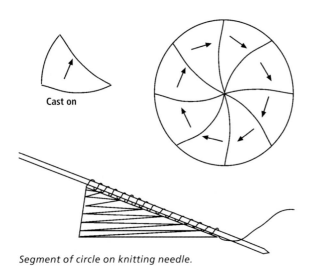

Cast on

*Segment of circle on knitting needle.*

## Circles and squares

Another way of forming circles, hexagons, octagons or squares is to knit them either from the centre out or from the outside edge in. Either way, you will need to work on four or five short double-ended needles at the centre when there are too few stitches for a circular needle.

This is fiddly knitting, but another great way of designing with stripes as they show up the direction so clearly. If you work from the centre outwards and increase, the way you increase will affect the structure and pattern. A single increase made always in the same position, perhaps on alternate rows, will naturally form a spiral pattern, in the same way that spirals are visible at the centre of a sunflower. This works particularly well with hexagonal shapes or octagons, increasing at six or eight regular points around the shape: work on three needles for a hexagon, knitting with the fourth, increasing at the beginning and centre of each row: the same goes for an octagon using four needles and knitting with the fifth. A 'yarn over' increase makes a decorative hole and also allows the knitting to expand easily.

This method can also be used in a square, although here you will need to increase every row for it to grow quickly enough to lie flat. If you make several of these shapes to be joined, perhaps for a bedspread, the spirals form a vigorous, lively pattern with lots of movement. If you want a calmer effect, you need to pair the increases: on a square shape, a double increase at each corner makes a regular, symmetrical shape. Regular increases around the circle can be used every four or six rows to make a circle with straight, radiating columns of stitches.

Of course any of these shapes can be worked from the outside inwards using double decreases. In my experience, decreases can be a little tighter than increases, restricting the movement of the fabric, so that as you draw near to the centre there is no room for the fabric to lie flat and it tends to start to poke up: a great design tool for the centre of a hat, but not so good for a mat. You can always stop short of the absolute centre and draw the stitches up by threading yarn through them on a sewing needle to fasten off.

Without even introducing colour, all the stitches described so far can be explored to make limitless textured patterns and effects. Stitches will show best in plain yarns, knitted to a fairly firm tension.

## Circle knitted in the round

Circles knitted in the round on double-ended needles, in stripes of two rows each colour, holding stitches on three needles, knitting with the fourth.

**Top left:** worked from the centre outwards with 6 pairs of increases every four rows, knitting into front and back of st to increase.

**Top right:** working in from the outside edge and decreasing towards the centre, with six pairs of decreases every 4th row: K2 tog paired with S1, K1, psso.

**Bottom left:** working from the outside inwards, with 6 single decreases on alternate rows.

**Bottom right:** working from the centre out, 6 single increases made with a 'yo'.

Single incs and decs create a swirling pattern.

## Squares knitted in the round

Squares knitted in the round on a set of five double-ended needles, in stripes of 2 rows each colour, using one needle for each side of the square, knitting with the fifth.

**Top left:** worked from the centre outwards, with a single increase (K into front and back of st) in 4 places, every row.

**Top right:** worked from the outside edge, with a single decrease in 4 places every row.

**Middle left:** worked from the centre outwards, with 4 double increases on alternate rows, made by picking up and knitting the stitch from the row below at the beginning and end of each needle.

**Middle right:** increasing from the centre outwards, this time knitting into the front and the back of the first and last stitch on each needle on alternate rows.

**Bottom left:** working from the outside in, decreasing at the beginning and end of each needle as follows: K2 tog, knit to last 2 sts, S1, K1, psso on alternate rows.

**Bottom right:** working from the outside in, decreasing at the beginning and end of each needle as follows: S1, K1, psso, knit to last 2 sts, K2 tog on alternate rows.

# CHAPTER 3

# Techniques

Study it as though it were totally unfamiliar.
2) Try to apply the principles of time and motion study. There are several thousand stitches
in most garments so even the slightest waste of energy or time in making a single stitch
soon adds up to an impressive total.
3) Study every detail connected with it. Study the yarn, the tools and the knitted fabrics.
Feel them draw the stitches. When knitting, listen to the click of the needles and notice the
pull of the yarn against stitches, needles and hands. Try to explain every change.
(4) Expend time liberally in the early stages, it pays in the end.

Extracts from *'Hints on learning knitting'* in Audrie Stratford, *Introducing Knitting* (1972)

There are numbers of demonstration videos available on the Internet showing different knitting techniques and instructions for particular stitches. There is a fund of knowledge out there, and it can be a useful way of learning, either as a beginner, or to discover new methods and techniques. The pace is usually just right for knitting along with: you can stop and start, watch again, and work at your own speed. The danger is that anyone can post one of these videos, and the unspoken message is that the way shown is the best method. There really is no official way of knitting; as I have discussed, techniques have varied through time and place, so who is to say what is right and what is wrong?

I don't believe in set rules for hand knitting. My approach is to aim for the simplest and most comfortable method for each individual, involving the shortest journey for the yarn and therefore the smallest movement of the hands. Some of the internet demonstrators leave no window of possibility that there might be a better way than the one they show, and I question the presumption that 'this is the way to do it'; to the viewer, some demonstrations look clumsy and laborious.

Through teaching knitting design workshops for over thirty years I have had time to observe many different ways of knitting and have learnt an enormous amount about different methods. I have been shown some invaluable tips, seen various ways of holding the needles for knitting right-handed, and different variations of 'continental' or left-handed knitting; there are different ways of holding the yarn originating in Germany, Scandinavia, Britain and America, and Eastern Europe. Even more unusual (to British knitters) are techniques from western Europe and South America discussed in Chapter 1, involving

*OPPOSITE PAGE:*
*Knitting tools: straight, circular and double-ended knitting needles, crochet hooks, stitch holders, cable stitch holders, and 'French' or cord knitters with different numbers of pegs.*

*Knitting with a yarn in either hand on a circular needle, with the yarn tensioned around the fourth fingers.*

carrying the yarn round the neck instead of holding it in the hand. Another method is to work in complete mirror-image to right-handed knitting, which is often the result of being left-handed and sitting opposite a right-handed knitter to learn. This is an equally valid method with an identical result, and if you can knit in either direction, you can always work on the right side of the knitting without ever having to turn at the end of the row; Elizabeth Zimmermann called this 'knitting back backwards'. I have read different opinions about the 'correct' way to knit, looked at photos and old books, and listened to experienced knitters. In Britain, the story is that the Victorians thought it looked more elegant to hold the needles underneath, like pens, so perhaps fashions have influenced methods as well as products. Everyone's hands are different, and many knitters have developed a speed in whatever method they have adopted and don't want to change. It is very difficult to alter an accustomed method.

It seems to me that the bottom line is to knit as efficiently as possible to suit yourself. Some of the knitting videos agree on this point at least. If you can sit comfortably, remain relaxed without straining your neck, shoulders, wrists or back and knit at a reasonable speed, there is not much wrong with the way you knit. If you cannot knit for long periods without becoming stiff or uncomfortable, if your hands travel unnecessary journeys to carry the yarn around the needles, and if you let go of the

*Holding the needles on top, near the working tips, with a yarn in either hand.*

*RIGHT: Making a knit stitch with the left-hand yarn in the 'continental' way.*

needles to do this, then it is definitely worth questioning and searching for a better, more efficient method.

If you analyse the journey of the yarn when knitting stitches from the left needle to the right in the 'normal' British way, the fact is that carrying the yarn in the right hand does entail a much longer journey than if it is held in the left hand. Changing from knit to purl within the row also means a lot of yarn movement for right-handed knitters; it has to travel round the tip of the right needle again and again, back and forth between the stitches as well as round the tip of the needle to make each stitch. If the yarn is held in the left hand, however, it slips through between the needles with almost no movement, making a knit 1, purl 1 rib almost as quick as plain knitting.

There cannot be any argument that the slowest method of knitting is to hold the needles way down the shafts far from the tips, and to let go of the needle to carry the yarn round; beginners often knit like this, understandably, as there is a lot of complicated coordination to learn involving different movements from each hand, needing a lot of control, which takes practice. If this is the way you knit, whether you are right-handed or left-handed, it is worth trying holding the needles on top, near to the points, not from underneath like a pen, holding the yarn in such a way that it runs through your hand freely under a tiny bit of tension without falling off. Both these factors minimise movement of the hands.

You could look at the 'fastest knitter' videos online to get an idea of how efficient hand knitting can be, and how little movement is needed from your hands. In 2010 the fastest knitter happens to be someone using the left-handed 'continental' method.

If you can see that there would be an advantage in speeding up your knitting, you could try this approach. You have to be determined in order to relearn something that has become a habit, and you have to be patient and willing to practise every day until it becomes natural. You may manage

to improve your present method enough to get a little more speed; this is up to you. I know people who have picked up one or two tips and managed to change enough to help them knit significantly faster, and others who have been determined and relearnt a completely different way; but again, you have to see the point in order to make the effort to change. Many people knit with unnecessary movement but with a terrific speed and efficiency, and may be content not to change.

When I teach beginners or children, I encourage people to pick up the yarn in whichever hand feels natural – no rules about right or left hand. Ideally if you can learn to knit with the yarn in either hand, you have an advantage: you are on the way to being able to knit fast in two-colour patterns, and to carry on knitting either way if one hand gets tired.

To sum up, everyone's hands are different, and different methods of knitting can work for different people. The main thing is to step back and take a look at the way you knit: to aim to knit efficiently with economy of movement, whether right- or left-handed, and to sit in a position that is not tensing your back, neck or shoulders. Knitting is supposed to be relaxing.

# CHAPTER 4

# COLOUR

> I want to try to convey to you that a sense of colour is not something you automatically
> know about; you discover and rediscover its secrets by playing with it and, above all,
> by constantly looking.
>
> Kaffe Fassett, *Glorious Knitting (1985)*

Working with colour opens up a whole world of more possibilities in knitting, both in creating patterns, geometric or free-form, and also in combining stitches and colours to get more subtle or intense effects. There are several ways of using colours to make different kinds of patterns in knitting, and they can also be combined in the same piece for different effects:

- The simplest colour patterning using one colour at a time has to be knitting **stripes**. This can be developed by using **slip stitches** for geometric, small or large-scale patterns while still working in stripes of single colours.
- **Intarsia** is to knit with several colours in a row, each having its own area, so still producing a single-thickness fabric, with the opportunity for free patterning.
- Using two or more yarns per row, each one travelling all the way across, is known as **Fair Isle** or **jacquard** knitting, resulting in (usually) smaller, geometric patterns and a thicker fabric.

OPPOSITE PAGE: *Clockwise from top left: 'poppy' design in Fair Isle technique with embossed textural stitches; intarsia design (colours used only in their own area); intarsia rainbow design; slip-stitch pattern (worked in stripes with slip stitches); and Fair Isle zigzag pattern.*

## Knitted Stripes

Horizontal stripes are the simplest form of pattern-making with different colours because you are following the direction of the knitting, changing colour at the beginning of a row. Stripes can be any number of rows wide, but if you are working back and forth, even numbers of rows are easier, as yarns can be left hanging at the end of the row and picked up again when needed. To work in an odd numbers of rows, or

*Simple stripes emphasize the direction of the knitting.*

Two-row stripes in (from left to right) stocking stitch, moss stitch, purl-side stocking stitch and garter stitch. Moss and garter stitch pull the fabric upwards.

Two-row stripes in a chequerboard of knit-facing and purl-facing stocking stitch, showing clear and blurred stripes.

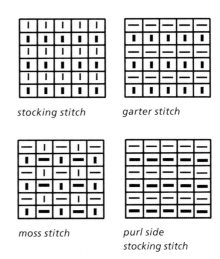

*stocking stitch*      *garter stitch*

*moss stitch*      *purl side
stocking stitch*

Striped stitch panels charts.

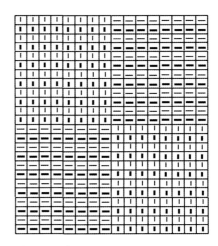

Chequerboard stripes chart.

change colour every row, the yarn may end up the wrong end of the row, so if you use a double-ended or circular needle, the stitches can be slid back to where the yarn is waiting, and the row knitted in the same direction again.

If you are knitting stripes in the round on several needles or a circular needle the number of rounds can be odd or even; the yarn will always be available when you get back to the beginning of the round. However, when you knit in the round, you are knitting a spiral, so there will always be a step up at the colour change. A thick yarn will make a bigger step and this will be more noticeable. It will also show more in narrow than in wide stripes. This is one of the few instances where circular knitting may not be the best way to knit, since by knitting back and forth you can match your stripes perfectly at the joins.

## Different stitches and mixing colour

Working stripes in stocking stitch gives a clean colour change on the knit side of the fabric, and a mixed or blurred colour change on the purl side. We are used to calling these differences 'right' and 'wrong' sides, but of course the different characteristics can be used as part of a design.

On the knit side of a stocking stitch fabric you are seeing the vertical sides of the knitted stitch, but on the purl side the horizontal top of the loop is linked across the loops from the next row, so the colours cross each other to make the blurred effect. If you want a soft, mixed effect from your stripes, the purl side of stocking stitch could be used, or a moss stitch, where stitches are alternately knitted and purled in each row. Moss stitch worked in one-row stripes blends the colours very subtly, and it also softens the edges of two-row stripes. Blocks of knit-side and purl-side stocking stitch or moss stitch can provide alternating clear and mixed stripes.

One-row stripes of garter stitch give a soft, mixed, tweedy effect, slightly different on each side, but if worked in two-row stripes, the stripes again have a clear-edged side and a blurred side

This contrast between clear colour change and mixed blended effects is a great tool in designing, if you think of mixing colours as if you were painting, breaking colours down into dots (stitches) rather as the French Impressionist painters did. Knitting only one colour per row is quite straightforward, but you can give the illusion of mixed colours. Some of the most basic stitches, that is moss stitch, garter stitch and a variety of slip stitches, can be worked in simple stripes with colours changing row by row, but the alternating knits, purls or slip stitches result in a textured 'dotty' effect of blended colours. In other words, while working in a simple way, the stitches will do the work of mixing the colours for you. So if you want to create an effect of a rich orange, you can use different shades such as an orangey-red and an orangey-yellow in this way, and the resulting colour blend will have more richness and interest than a single colour on its own.

Why bother going to the trouble of mixing colours in the knitting when so many shades are available to buy? If you make something by hand, you have the opportunity to make it interesting both from a distance, and with increasing interest and detail from close up. Often in mass-produced clothes, a design can read well from a distance but become disappointingly flat as you get closer. Yarns, particularly wools, have such richness of colour it is a pleasure to be

*One-row stripes mix the colours even more. From top, moss stitch, stocking stitch and garter stitch.*

able to play with this in the form of stitches. Think of the subtlety of woven tapestry, where again colours can be 'built' in amazingly rich effects in the weaving, and grab the chance to do the same in knitting.

## Directions

Stripes are a great tool in pattern-making, as they visually reinforce the direction of the rows, so can be used very effectively if you are knitting in different directions. Knitting flat pieces from the centre outwards (or the outside edge inwards) in a square or circular shape will emphasize that shape and construction with stripes radiating inwards or outwards. This is simple and obvious, but just try it: stripes travelling in different directions can be stunning. Where the knitting construction is already interesting, stripes make a strong impact and the simplicity can become sophisticated.

**Short-row wavy textures worked on 27 sts.**

This uses short rows to distort the fabric.

Using col A, P1 row, K1 row.

Start short-row shaping, with purl-side facing. It looks similar to 'wavy welting' (*see* pages 61), but is formed differently.

(To prevent holes where you turn in the short rows, see Chapter 6.)

Using col B, * K9, turn; S1, P7, turn; S1, K6, turn; S1, P5, turn; S1, K4, turn; S1, P3, turn; S1, K3, turn; S1, P4, turn; S1, K5, turn; S1, P6, turn; S1, K7, turn; S1, P8, turn, K9 *. Rep from * to * all along the row for each group of 9 sts.

Break off yarn, and slide needles back to col A.

**Row 1** Knit.

**Row 2** Knit.

**Row 3** Purl.

**Row 4** Knit.

Change to col C, K5, turn; S1, P4, turn; K4, turn; S1, P3, turn; K3, turn; S1, P2, turn; K4, turn; S1, P3, turn; K5. Work from * to * to last 4 sts.

K4 turn; P4, turn; K3 turn; P3, turn; S1, K2, turn; P3, turn; S1, K2, turn; P4, turn; S1, K3.

Break off yarn, slide sts back to col A.

**Row 1** Knit.

**Row 2** Knit.

**Row 3** Purl.

**Row 4** Knit.

Rep these 8 rows changing colours as you want.

If you want your design to have vertical or diagonal stripes, it is worth considering changing the direction of the knitting so you can still knit straightforward horizontal stripes with the rows travelling across. If the piece is knitted sideways, the stripes appear vertical, saving you the complication of having to use several colours in a row. Similarly, for diagonal stripes, if you knit from the bottom edge with lots of colours, again you have the problem of several balls of yarn travelling in each row, but you could build the shape by knitting it diagonally, starting in the corner so that the rows slope, increasing at either end of the row until you have enough stitches, then decreasing at one or both edges to make the shape you want, with the stripes following the rows. Always search for the easiest way to get the result you want.

## Knitting curves

Because knitted fabric is basically a grid of horizontal rows and vertical columns, it makes it difficult to create convincing curves unless you are working at a very fine gauge or tension and with large curves: this is immediately evident if you work out a curved design on squared paper. Try drawing a circle on a grid. Larger squares give jerky edges, but on a fine scale with small squares the illusion of a curve is more successful. However, there are some simple ways to make patterns that bend and curve naturally by changing the structure of the knitted rows.

### Short rows

Rather than knitting all the way across the row, you can turn and work back at any point (*see* Chapter 6). This makes the knitted fabric grow unevenly, and it can be controlled to make practical shaping such as 'darts' or the heel on a sock, or it can be used to create any kind of random texture. If you work in stripes, this emphasizes the shaping, and can create fluid curve and wave effects, following the movement of the rows of knitting.

### Increasing and decreasing within the rows

Increasing and decreasing within the row can also distort the fabric, but whereas in 'short-row' knitting the stitches are being pushed off their regular horizontal path and the extra rows push the stitches to make them wave up and down, in this case they are being pushed sideways off the vertical by the movement of the stitches, although this affects the rows as well. The rows are worked all the way across, but the stitches begin to travel diagonally. This diagonal movement also makes the fabric tilt, so playing with colour changes make stripes that will tilt, wave or zigzag accordingly.

## Moss stitch zigzag

This has more stitches between the increases and decreases, and the 2-row coloured stripes are blurred and softened by the moss stitch. The increases and decreases mean that the knits and purls change position every row, so need to be watched to keep the moss stitch pattern regular.

*Cast on a multiple of 34 sts.*

**Row 1** * Knit into front and back of stitch, moss stitch 14, S1, K1, psso, K2 tog, moss stitch 14, knit into front and back of stitch *; rep from * to * for more zigzags.
Row 2) Moss stitch 16, P2, moss stitch 16.
Rep these 2 rows.

## Wavy welting stitch

In this sample, the colours change on rows 1 and 3. Rows 1 and 2 make the narrow stocking stitch stripe, and rows 3–6 are the purl-facing 'ridge'. The effect is similar to short-row waves: *see* page 60.

*Cast on a multiple of 9 sts and knit 2 rows, then start pattern.*

**Row 1** * K2 tog, K1, K into front and back of next st, K into front and back of next st, K2, S1, K1, psso. Rep from * to *.
**Row 2** Purl.
**Row 3** As row 1.
**Row 4** Knit.
**Row 5** Knit.
**Row 6** Purl.
Repeat these 6 rows.

*Wavy welting chart.*

*Moss stitch zigzag chart.*

*Big wave pattern, with more increases and decreases grouped together and more stitches between the shapings.*

*Big wave pattern chart.*

## Slip Stitches

Still using one colour per row but working in stripes, if you slip stitches from the left needle to the right needle instead of knitting them, different colours are pulled across each other and can be made into small textured patterns. This doesn't have to be small scale; bold designs are equally possible, and there can be a freedom of movement of groups of stitches to make diagonal or other effects across the surface of the knitting. In stocking stitch the usually smooth surface will be hitched up by the slip stitches, which again can make geometric patterns and distort the colours. If garter stitch is incorporated, a much more textured effect is achieved. Two things happen to the character of the knitted fabric in slip stitches:

- The width will pull in very slightly and will have a little less stretch than usual, as the yarn travels straight across behind each slipped stitch.
- The length will also be pulled up slightly by the slipped stitches, so the knitting grows more slowly. This is most noticeable when a lot of stitches are slipped; for example, 'tweed stitch' (where you slip alternate stitches) naturally grows half as quickly as normal knitting as only half the stitches are worked in each row.

As well as being used for decorative patterns and mixing colours (as described earlier), slip-stitch knitting is functional and can be used to advantage when a slightly thicker and less stretchy fabric is needed, as described in Chapter 2.

## Fair Isle Knitting

Two-colour knitting (often called Fair Isle as it was used traditionally on the Scottish islands, and sometimes called jacquard) is most suited to making smallish repeated patterns, with colours changing every few stitches, and both yarns being carried or woven along the back of the row. This results in a thicker and less stretchy fabric than single-yarn knitting because of the double layer, and the yarn that is travelling at the back has a tendency to lie straight and limit the stretch. You could use as many colours as you like, but with more than two it becomes more difficult to manage, and correspondingly bulkier.

In order to manage the different yarns as you knit, they can be held over different fingers to keep them separate, or very efficiently (when you have mastered it) using both hands, holding the yarns one in each hand: knitting right-handed with one colour and left-handed with the other. If you intend to do much of this type of knitting, it is really worth learning this as it is then possible to weave the colours on the back to prevent long strands with a simple 'twiddle' – no twisting or tangling involved – and to knit almost as fast as with a single yarn. Whichever hand you usually use to hold the yarn, practise knitting some plain stocking stitch with the other hand until it becomes comfortable, and then try with two hands. 'Stranding' and 'weaving' the thread that is not being knitted have different effects. In 'stranding', the yarn is simply carried straight across the back of the knitting so that it floats free. In 'weaving', not only is the yarn linked in with the yarn that is knitting, making it firmer and less likely to catch and pull, but it also travels up and down rather than straight across, allowing for more stretch.

# Fair Isle knitting

There are four movements to learn:

(1)     Knit with right hand, weave in with left hand.

(2)     Knit with left hand, weave in with right hand.

(3)     Purl with right hand, weave in with left hand.

(4)     Purl with left hand, weave in with right hand.

## Instructions in detail

(Rep (a) and (b) along the row in each case)

(1) Knit row, RH knitting, LH weaving:

(a) K1 with RH, holding LH yarn below.

(b) K next st with RH, holding LH yarn above.

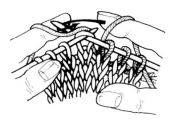

(2) Knit row, LH knitting, RH weaving:

(a) K1 with LH.

(b) Needle in next st: RH yarn over as if to knit, LH yarn over. RH yarn off, and make stitch (say 'over, over, off, through').

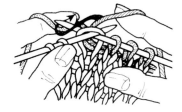

(3) Purl row, RH purling, LH weaving:

(a) P1 with RH, holding LH yarn below.

(b) Purl next st with RH, holding LH yarn above.

(4) Purl row, LH purling, RH weaving:

(a) P1 with LH (note: yarn must go in same direction over needle as it does in RH purling).

(b) Needle in next st, RH yarn under needle, LH yarn over needle, RH yarn off, and make st (say 'under, over, off, through').

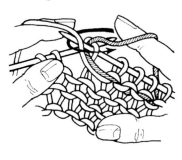

Use the dominant colour in your more comfortable hand. This method is also invaluable for weaving in loose ends, holding them in the left hand and weaving up and down in the same way.

*Fair Isle knitting using two colours per row, with the spare yarn woven on the back, in an up and down movement (not twisted).*

## Slip stitch patterns

All samples are knitted in two-row stripes, cols A and B, but the stripes are disguised by slipping the stitches. There is enormous scope for different patterns and textures using this method, but they are all simple to knit as only one colour is used at a time.

Slip stitches have a tendency to pull the fabric in widthways and up lengthways, making a thicker texture than plain knitting. The amount they pull in depends on how many stitches are slipped; for example, the first sample has alternate stitches slipped on every row, whereas others have fewer slipped stitches with plain rows between slipped rows, so do not pull up or inwards so much.

### a) Coloured tweed stitch

*Cast on an odd no of sts.*

**Row 1** (Right side) Using col A, K1 * yf, S1 p-wise, yb, K1; rep from * to end, K1.

**Row 2** Using col A, P2 * yb, S1 p-wise, yf, P1; rep from * to last st, P1.

**Row 3** Using col B, as row 1.

**Row 4** Using col B, as row 2.

These 4 rows form the pattern.

Half the stitches are slipped in this stitch so it grows slowly and pulls in (and up)

A band of 2- row stripes is followed by:

### b) Vertical stripes

*Cast on an even no of sts.*

**Row 1** Using col A, K3, S2, * K2, S2 *; rep from * to * to last 3 sts, K3.

**Row 2** Using col A, P3, S2, * P2, S2 *; rep from * to * to last 3 sts, P3.

**Row 3** Using col B, K1, S2, * K2, S2 *; rep from * to * to last st, K1.

**Row 4** Using col B, P1, S2, * P2, S2 *; rep from * to * to last st, P1.

Half the stitches are slipped in this stitch so it grows slowly and pulls in (and up).

A band of 2- row stripes is followed by:

### c) Diagonal garter stripe slip stitch

This stitch only slips 1 out of 3 sts, so it doesn't pull in as much as the previous patterns. It is also garter stitch rather than stocking stitch, so is thicker than before.

Always carry yarn on wrong side.

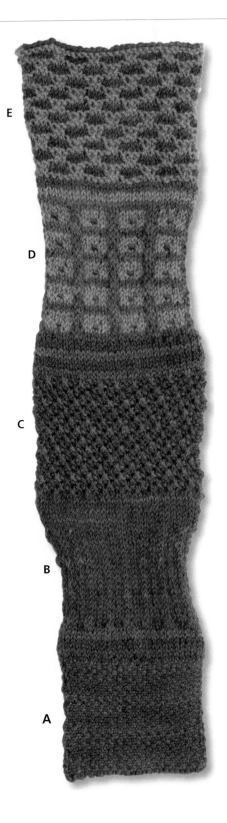

Cast on a_multiple of 3 sts + 2 extra.

**Row 1** (Right side) Using col A, K3, S1, * K2, S1 *; rep from * to * to last st, K1.

**Row 2** Using col A, K1 * S1, K2 *; rep from * to * to last st, K1.

**Row 3** Using col B, K2 * S1, K2 *; rep from * to * to end.

**Row 4** Using col B, as row 3.

**Row 5** Using col A, as row 2.

**Row 6** Using col A, as row 1.

**Row 7** Using col B, as row 1.

**Row 8** Using col B, as row 2.

**Row 9** Using col A, as row 3.

**Row 10** Using col A, as row 3.

**Row 11** Using col B, as row 2.

**Row 12** Using col B, as row 1.

### d) Grid pattern

*Cast on a multiple of 7 sts + 4 extra.*

Always carry the yarn on the wrong side.

**Row 1** (Right side) Using col A (darker colour), knit.

**Row 2** Using col A, purl.

**Row 3** Using col B, K1, S2 * K5, S2 *; rep from * to * to last st, K1.

**Row 4** Using col B, P1, S2 * P5, S2 *; rep from * to * to last st, P1.

**Row 5** Using col A, K3, * S2, K1, S2, K2 *; rep from * to * to last st, K1.

**Row 6** Using col A, P3, * S2, K1, S2, P2 *; rep from * to * to last st, P1.

**Row 7** As row 3.

**Row 8** As row 4.

### e) Spotty pattern

This only slips 2 sts out of every 6, so again does not pull in very much.

*Cast on a multiple of 6 sts + 2 extra.*

**Row 1** Using col A (lighter colour), knit.

**Row 2** Using col A, knit.

**Row 3** Using col B, K3 * S2, K4 *; rep from * to * to last 3 sts, K3.

**Row 4** Using col B, P3 * S2, P4 *; rep from * to * to last 3 sts, P3.

**Row 5** As row 1.

**Row 6** As row 2.

**Row 7** Using col B, * S2, K4 *; rep from * to * to last 2 sts, S2.

**Row 8** Using col B, * S2, P4 *; rep from * to * to last 2 sts, S2.

Slip-stitch charts.

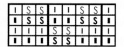

*A. tweed stitch*

*B. vertical stripes*

*C. diagonal garter stitch*

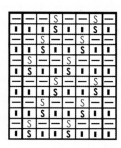

*D. grid pattern*

*E. spotty pattern*

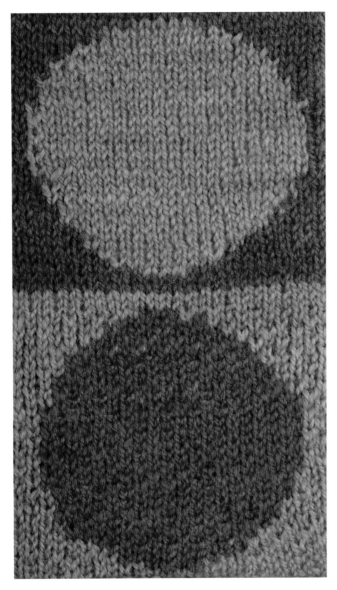

*Circles pattern knitted in intarsia (top), which gives a clearer colour than Fair Isle (bottom), where the opposite colours show slightly from being woven across the back.*

*Squares pattern knitted in intarsia (top, larger squares) and Fair Isle (bottom).*

## Intarsia Knitting

A completely different method, giving more freedom in the range of potential designs, is intarsia knitting, which lets each colour travel over its own area, linking with the neighbouring colour but making a single-weight fabric. This may mean working with several different balls of yarn in each row, a separate ball for each colour, so it is not as easy to get into a rhythm and flow in the action of knitting as it is with a single or two-colour regular pattern, but is more appropriate for freer, bolder and more sweeping colour designs. Rather than working with complete balls of yarn, you can wind off small amounts of each colour if only a little is to be used, keeping them on a piece of card or special holder to prevent them unravelling; this means that each colour can hang free and not tangle with its neighbour.

## Mixing Methods

All these different methods of using colour have been described separately, but of course mix them up – use whatever is practical. If there are some small dots in a multicoloured pattern, the dot-colours can be individual balls of yarn; they don't need to travel all across the row. However, it is really important to think about the thickness and weight of the fabric if you are going to use different methods as you may end up with thick, lumpy areas and other thinner patches. This is fine as long as it looks and feels balanced and intentional.

## Designing with Colour

Although such a variety of yarn is now available to buy, it's still not always possible to find the exact colours you want for a design. If you find this frustrating and would like more choice, you could try dyeing your own yarns. You may like to try anyway; it opens up another whole world of creating pattern and colour in design, both in the range of colours you can mix and the way you apply colour to the yarn. It is like the difference between mixing your own paints instead of using them straight out of a tube or can; there is a sense of

*Colour study of autumn leaves: yarns, yarn winding and knitted sample. A spiky, pointed stitch pattern was suggested by the leaf shapes.*

freedom in being able to design your own colours. As well as giving you a much wider range, you can play with the way the yarn absorbs the colour by blending or shading, or tie-dyeing to make more definite patterns on the actual thread, to give particular effects in the knitting.

How you decide what colours to use and how to combine them is sometimes daunting: where to start? You may know what colours you like, but when you try and use them in knitting, they don't seem to work in the way you want them to. Some people have a natural confidence in using colours together that seems to 'work', but what does that mean? Are certain combinations of colours right and others wrong, as in the old saying 'blue and green should never be seen'? Are there really rules, or are some colour groupings generally more popular than others? Liking colour combinations is personal; different people like different types of colour: perhaps bright colours with strong contrasts or with close clashes – think of Mexican designs using strong pinks, oranges and yellows. Other people find interest in soft, subtle colours, perhaps the colours of pebbles on a beach,

variations on greys and whites, ranging from creamy-white to bluey-white, browny-grey to pewter. Another example of more subtle colouring could be a crowd scene on a winter day in northern Europe: shades of greys and browns with perhaps tiny amounts of brightness. The light changes throughout different parts of the world as you move closer to or further from the equator, and softer colours seem more natural to cooler regions, with brighter light and stronger colours more at home in hotter climates. However, where you live does not have to govern your preferences: living in a grey, cold environment could promote a desire for hot, rich, vibrant colours.

Grey, black and monotone shades do not have to be quiet and dull either. A bold effect can be produced even when colours are subtle in their differing shades by varying the light and dark to extremes, so that the result is still strong and startling: for instance shades of white and off-whites used with different shades of black: browny-black, bluey-black and greeny-black will be strong and bold because of the tonal contrast.

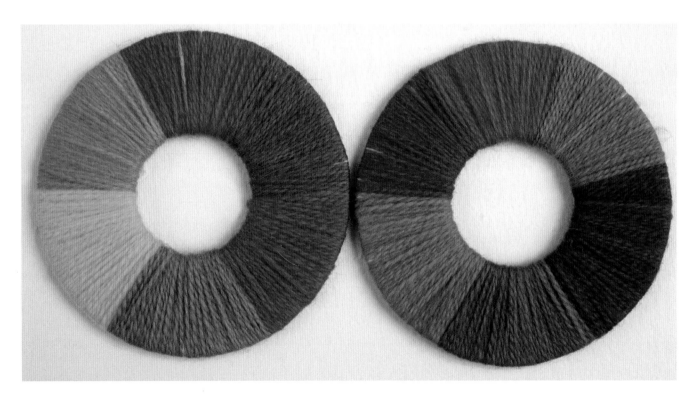

*Colour wheels*
*Left: acid dyes on wool using the three primary colours, red, blue and yellow, and the secondary colours mixed from these to make purple, green and orange. Right: acid dyes mixed to give softer variations on primary and secondary colours.*

# Colour theory

The colour wheel is used as a way of trying to explain how colours work. It illustrates the three primary or 'pure' colours – red, blue and yellow – mixing them in pairs to get 'secondary' colours – purple, green and orange. The greatest contrasts are then between a primary colour and its 'opposite' secondary: red opposed to green, blue to orange, and yellow to purple. The contrast is there because there is no common link between these opposites: green is a mixture of blue and yellow so red plays no part in green – it is as far removed as possible. At their purest these contrasts can be harsh or dazzling, but if you start to play with colour mixes by making them 'impure', they can be toned down and softened, changing the contrast into something gentler and richer. For instance, instead of a pure red, mix an earthy terracotta red, and use it with a blue-green or a yellow-green, and the vigour is taken out of the contrast, but a relationship is introduced: each shade contains a small amount of the others, leaving something more mellow but still with vibrancy. Whatever result you want or combinations of colours you enjoy is up to you, and by being aware and questioning what you see, you can increase your ability to use colour in design.

Colour theory in the form of the colour wheel can be helpful in understanding certain things about colour, but is not the only guide to designing. It is a scientific approach, not a personal one, and it is our own reaction to colour that makes individuality in designing. The outspoken gardener and writer Christopher Lloyd had strong opinions on designing with colour:

> But just how are we supposed to use the Colour Wheel? I can well see that diametrically opposed colours are as different as colours can be and that adjacent colours have much in common, but what then? Are there colours that we must not use together? I think not. Well-handled (i.e. handled by me), any two colours can be pleasingly juxtaposed. (I'm still taking about plants, though I believe that much the same is true of fabrics.)
>
> Christopher Lloyd, gardener and writer, *Cuttings* (2007)

Being aware of the subtleties of colours in nature or our surroundings, and how to translate colours you have seen into a design, is a more creative approach than following rules, but it needs practice in looking and in consciously noticing and seeing, and understanding how to develop what you have seen into a design.

Another aspect of colour in design is that certain colour combinations can produce strong associations and memories, rather like scents or sounds. It could be as random as reminding you of a school uniform, or perhaps of food, or a memory of a particular landscape. Certain colour combinations can conjure up a period of time, a style of painting or an era in fashion. Groups of colours can have strong effects on emotions in the same way as hearing a piece of music associated with an important event. Colours can be gentle and soothing – perhaps spring green in a beech wood with soft shadows. They can be rich and delicious as good chocolate, sumptuous velvets in reds and golds, or autumn colours in a forest. Colours can be bright and startling; think of exotic bird feathers and markings, or bright and shocking, attracting attention, as in advertising and in the media. The colour red always makes an impact; we have a basic human reaction to red, using it to denote danger and to attract attention. On the other hand, greens can be soothing, yellows cheerful. Take some time to examine how you respond

*Wool dyed in acid dyes, playing with the idea of a main colour in several shades and variations enlivened and contrasted with small amounts of its almost-complementary colour: so shades of green with a touch of red, shades of red with a bright greeny-blue, shades of blue with orangey-rust, shades of purple with yellow and gold.*

*A colour exercise working from pebbles with subtle differences in the grey colourings and the occasional stripe. The yarn winding looks at the proportions of the colours, and the knitted sample follows the proportions in knitted stripes, with a literal interpretation of the 'X' pattern.*

to colours; everyone is affected in some way. Colour plays a more dominant role for some people than others; in extreme cases people with the condition of colour synaesthesia see numbers or hear words in colour. This is an intense reaction and everyone has different degrees of sensitivity to colour, but we can all train ourselves to be more colour-aware.

## Interpreting colours seen

If you are unsure how take the plunge and start combining colours, it is easy to copy someone else's suggestions or colours used in another medium. Following a knitting pattern can be very rewarding, but the first real step towards designing is to start asking questions. Don't just accept someone else's choice unthinkingly. Have you ever been aware that you are not really satisfied with the colours you have used – there is something about the combination of colours that is bothering you?

One step forward might be to try copying patterns seen in other crafts: patterns on pots, in prints, or tiles. Although this is a good source of ideas for colour and pattern, again it may not be as simple as it seems to get a satisfactory result. It needs acute awareness: if the colours are even slightly different to the original colours seen, the effect will not be the same. Imagine a piece of vintage Fair Isle knitting: the colours are probably muted and soft. It may not be possible to find identical colours to work with, but if approximate colours are chosen, the result can miss the mark altogether and look brash, hard and crude compared with the original. This is inadvertently illustrated in knitting books with the theme of showing period pieces by knitting and translating them with modern yarns into a contemporary design. It happens with reproductions in other fields too: an old Roman mosaic would have soft, subtle colours, with each piece of tile varying slightly from others, whereas a modern copy with contemporary materials may not have the same subtlety of shading, and the result can be hard and flat in comparison. There is nothing wrong with hard, flat colours, in mosaic, knitting, or anything else, as long as it is what is intended and the difference is noticed. The point is to be aware and question what you do or don't like about colours, and try and understand why.

So … what to do? Where to start? How to arrive at colours you like? One simple way of sorting colours is to play with balls of yarn, arranging them so you can see different amounts (proportions) and rearranging to see how different colours change according to the colour they are next to, and to try to assess your own reactions to the different arrangements. This is rather approximate, but if you already have a collection of yarns, it is a way of looking at how the value of each colour can be changed by what you put it next to, and how different proportions change the whole balance.

## Colour exercise

Here is a simple but more thorough exercise to try, needing no special equipment apart from a collection of coloured yarns. All it needs is time: if you are not used to spending time designing, but used to plunging straight into a ready-made knitting pattern, it may seem daunting or wasteful to put off the knitting moment, but in the end time will be saved, and there will be a much better chance of a successful design than starting knitting with a vague idea that you can't really assess until you have done a lot of the knitting.

First of all, find something to work from: a photo or painting or object, a view from a window, containing a group of colours that you find stimulating to use as 'source material'. This is important; it has to be something that really grabs your imagination and excites you, even if it is as mundane as a brick wall (which may well contain many colours when you start to really look). If you have been trained in art or enjoy painting or using colours, you know that making a colour study of what you have seen helps you to look more carefully and to analyse the colours. This is a useful first step. However, the following simple exercises and rules can be followed whether or not you have any particular training or artistic skill, or any ability to draw or paint with colour, as they can be worked directly with coloured yarns.

**Step 1**
Find your source material to work from. It might be something you have seen in your surroundings, or in a picture or photo. It is the combination that is important: if you think of an isolated colour you like, this needs to be seen in context as it can lose its power or appeal in different environments or groupings. If you have a favourite blue, perhaps lapis lazuli, is it in a piece of jewellery, perhaps in a gold setting? Colours change absolutely depending on what they are seen against, so that your same blue will look quite different against silver, red, green or anything else. This is why the first step has to be to find a colour in context, or a group of colours that excite you.

## Step 2

Look at the proportions of colours that make up the area that attracts you. There may be a lot of quiet colours and a small amount of your favourite, or a brilliant stripe or patch of a colour.

## Step 3

Find some coloured yarns as close as possible to the colours you are studying. If they do not match exactly, try and break down the unmatched colour into component parts or colours as near as possible that could be mixed to give the same effect. If it is a green, choose several shades of bluey-green, yellow-green, browny-green or whatever, as near as possible, and use them all in single strands.

## Step 4

Cut a piece of card about 8cm (3in) by 3cm (1in) (the size is approximate), and wrap your yarns closely in single threads in bands along the strip of card, starting at one end, covering it completely in a single layer. A strip of double-sided sticky tape on the reverse will help to hold the ends firmly, or you can trap the ends with small slits in the card. Work in stripes

*Colour exercise taken from autumn trees: although the tree colours are so vivid, the dramatic contrast is in the dark trunks and the light frosty green strip of grass.*

of the proportions of the colours you are looking at, following the colours as they move from one to another, recording what each colour is next to. If one area of colour is twice as big as another, make a stripe twice as wide. If you need to mix your yarns to achieve an effect, use two or three colours in stripes of one strand at a time.

When you have finished, put the strip of card and the original inspiration, (a photo if that is what you are working from) on a wall or somewhere so you can stand back and look from a distance, and judge whether you have got a close interpretation, and more importantly, whether your yarn winding stripes have the same interest and excitement in colour combinations and proportions as the original source material. If not, try and work out why not: whether the relationship of the colours is different, or the proportions.

Keep standing back to compare your colours with your original source material. Once you feel you are progressing towards an accurate translation, the next step is to start knitting samples or small pieces where you play with the colours to move towards a design. At this stage, it can help to take some short cuts and either sketch out an idea on paper, or if it is difficult to get the same intensity of colour as the yarns you are working with, then try torn coloured paper and make a collage. You could use the actual yarns in solid blocks, wound onto small pieces of card covering the card completely, and move these around into a design.

A good size for a knitted sample would be at least 10cm (4in); anything smaller and you don't get enough to judge how it would look on a larger scale. At the simplest level, you can translate your striped piece of card into a striped piece of knitting, keeping the proportions of colours the same but perhaps introducing different textures and stitches. Or you can try something different, making the smallest stripes into dots or specks of colour, perhaps in slip stitches as suggested earlier. The most difficult aspect of all this is to keep it simple, and a simple design is often more successful than something complicated. Why is it so difficult to keep simple? Probably partly because knitting is slow and you can easily become bored repeating the same thing for too long; it's more interesting to keep varying the stitch or the colour. But you really can't judge the result from a small piece of knitting that keeps changing ideas every few rows; you need to knit enough to stand back and analyse the result.

Here is another short cut: if you have knitted a small sample, use a couple of small mirrors or mirror tiles held at right angles on two sides of your knitted piece to enlarge it. This will give you a fair impression of a larger piece, even though it is then in mirror image. Alternatively, scan it into your computer and put it

*A colour exercise working from grey-leafed plants and flowers on gravel, using a modular knitting stitch to represent the clumps of individual plants.*

into repeat to get the effect of a larger piece. Save time wherever you can – knitting takes long enough, and any tool that speeds up the decision-making process is helpful. Again, keep standing back and looking from a distance. You are working with your knitting so closely, it is often a complete surprise to see it from further away. Pin it up somewhere so you can see it as you walk past, and keep looking critically and trying to find out what you like and what you are not happy with.

Each time you do this exercise you will become more aware of how colours work together and how to alter proportions to get the results you want.

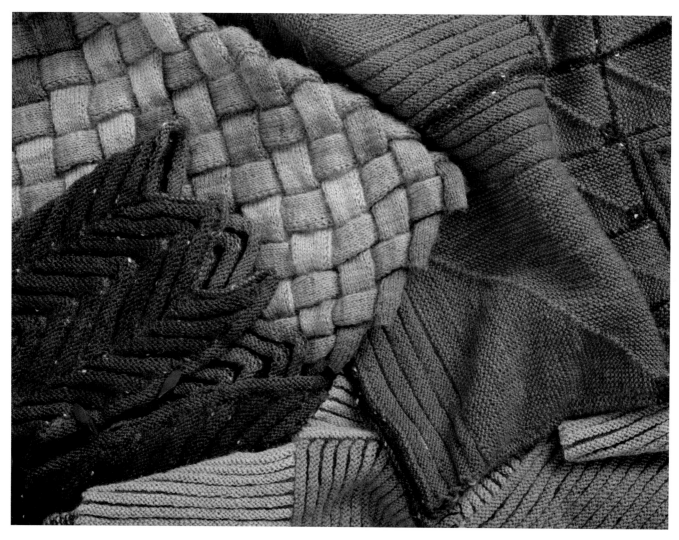

*A selection of knitting showing the characteristic subtle colour variation in hand-dyed wools.*

## Dyeing Yarn

Wool is a protein fibre, and can be dyed with 'acid dye', as can silk. Cotton, hemp, linen and other vegetable fibres need a different family of dyes called 'Reactive', often sold under the brand name Procion, although some Procions can also be used for silk. Both acid and Procion dyes, known as 'chemical' dyes, can be bought in powdered form, and diluted in a solution with water, and fixed onto the yarn with the addition a fixing agent: acetic acid (vinegar) for wool, and an alkaline for cotton, usually salt and (very dilute) caustic soda. Suppliers of yarn dyes supply instructions with their dyes and often sell small starter kits, so the following is only a general outline of the method, and advice on colour mixing and special effects.

There are different ways of applying the dye to the yarn, including painting it on and heating with a microwave, but basically the dye (which is manufactured in powder form) needs to combine with water to penetrate the yarn. This is not like painting onto fabric; 'dyeing' as described here combines colour with the fibre in a permanent way. There is also a group of dyes known as 'pigment' dyes which sit on the surface of the fibre and gradually wear off – for example Indigo dye, which gives the famous denim blue, and fades with wear and washing. But acid and Procion dyes penetrate into the fibre.

For a straightforward plain, even colour, the yarn needs to be in a hank (not a ball), so the dye can access it easily, and it needs to be prepared for dyeing in two ways: firstly it has to be tied at intervals on the hank to prevent tangling, and secondly any dressing or oil must be removed so the dye can penetrate properly. Try to obtain your yarn in a hank or skein. Some mail order companies and suppliers sell it in this way in its natural colour, or you may have access to handspun yarn. If this is not possible and you want to use yarn from a ball or cone you have already, this is the way to prepare it:

- Keep track of the first end by tying it loosely to a fixed point, which may be on a skein-holder, a chair back or the hands of a willing friend. Wind it round your chosen object or winder until you get to the second end, then twist this together with the first end, take each round the skein so the ends enclose the skein, and tie together loosely.

- Next, tie the skein with short lengths of string. This is essential to prevent it tangling. Cut three lengths of string or something strong about 42cm (16in) long, and tie in three evenly spaced places by taking the tie around the outside, then splitting the hank, passing the ends of the tie through the middle so they cross, passing them round the rest of the hank in a figure of eight and tying together firmly.

- This crossover prevents the ties sliding along the hank during dyeing and all ending up in one place.

- Next, weigh the yarn, using kitchen scales to be as precise as possible. This is essential as every other ingredient is worked out according to this weight. It means that you will be able to repeat the same colour shade again on any weight of yarn.

- Now wet the yarn, and if it is oily or treated with any kind of finish, wash it first. Fill a bucket or bowl with hand-hot water and a little detergent, hold the hank by one of the ties, and dip it repeatedly up and down into the hot water. Don't mash it about in the water, just dip repeatedly: too much movement can encourage some yarns to tangle or even worse, to felt. Certain types of wool felt when agitated in water, and the process is irreversible: the fibres lock together, shrinking and linking into a felted fabric. Fine if you are making felt; impossible if you want to separate the yarn threads later for knitting.

- Squeeze the yarn carefully without wringing or twisting, and rinse in warm water.

- Go back to your dye instructions and work out how much water you need for the weight of your yarn, and how much dye to get the depth of colour you want. The amount of water needs to allow room for the yarn to move about freely and the dye to penetrate evenly.

*Yarn prepared for dyeing, with the ends tied together.*

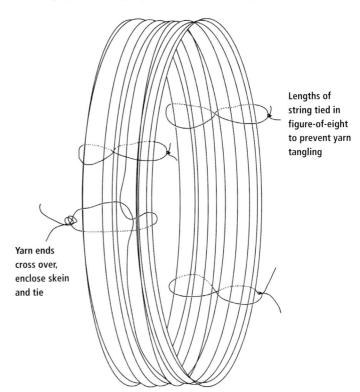

Lengths of string tied in figure-of-eight to prevent yarn tangling

Yarn ends cross over, enclose skein and tie

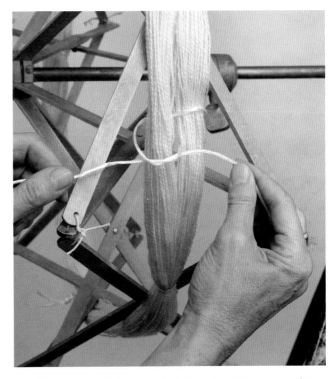

*Inserting 'ties' loosely into a skein before dyeing to prevent the yarn from tangling.*

If you are starting with a dyeing kit, you will be given some basic information for the strength of dye per 100g (3¹/2oz) of yarn, and the manufacturer may recommend wearing a mask if the dye is in powder form. In any event always mix dyes in a well-ventilated room. It is also a good idea to cover all adjacent surfaces as grains of dye can travel and stain whatever they touch. Rubber gloves are also useful if you don t want coloured hands. Always read and follow the safety instructions provided by your dye manufacturer.

## Getting started

A simple way to start is to have the three primary colours – red, yellow and blue – plus perhaps a black or brown which gives extra scope in adjusting and toning down these colours in mixes. If you are prepared to experiment and do some trials, you can build up a range of your own colours from these basics. You could start with trying out each colour on its own, say 2g

(¹/16oz ) of dye per 100g (3¹/2oz) of yarn from each primary colour so you have the three basic colours to refer to. Next you could mix equal amounts, for example 1 part yellow + 1 part blue to make green, and so on to mix the secondary colours. If you want to tone down the brightness, add a little black or brown and see what happens, but keep a record of the amount: write it down. You will soon begin to see how to adjust the colours to what you want. You may find one primary is stronger than another, so to make an effect, you have to add less in proportion. I find with acid dyes on wool that yellow needs a larger proportion to have an impact, and a very little red goes a long way. Tiny amounts of black or brown will make a huge difference. Black dye on its own needs at least 2 per cent strength (2g per 100g (¹/16oz per 3¹/2oz) of yarn to make a deep black; anything less gives a gentler charcoal, and used in very small amounts it gives warm grey. Sometimes, If not all the dye has been absorbed, you can get interesting results by dipping fresh wool in it; for instance, with acid black you can often dye a warm yellowy-beige in the remaining  exhaust  dye.

*Wool dyed in acid dyes, using a basic range red, blue, yellow, navy, brown and black: all hand-dyed yarns shown use these six shades.*

If you are working with powdered dye, it needs to be dissolved in a small amount of water first so that it spreads evenly in the dye bath. Powdered dye is difficult to measure accurately if you are dyeing small amounts of yarn, although teaspoon measures are given in your manufacturer's instructions for different weights. However, rather than trying to measure small fractions of a gram or ounce, it is easier to make it into a solution with some water and use a syringe to measure it (instructions and syringe are usually supplied with the dyes).

Some dyes need heat to work, and others can be used warm or tepid in a plastic container. If you need to heat it, you can use any cooking container (that is no longer used for cooking), or buy a custom-made stainless steel container. Some metals affect the colour of the dye, or are not suited to the acid or alkali added, so stainless steel is ideal.

Dyeing wool with acid dye, or cotton with Procion, takes about an hour, by which time the dye has been absorbed by the yarn, and in the case of the wool, the water is left almost clear. Wool absorbs dye much more readily than vegetable fibres do, so you would expect there to be dye remaining in the water after dyeing cotton, linen or hemp.

Finally, rinse the yarn according to the instructions, and hang to drip dry. When the yarn is completely dry, put your hands inside the skein and beat them firmly outwards several times to stretch out and separate the threads. Do this several times to free any tangles before you wind it down into a ball for knitting.

## Natural dyes

'Natural' dyes work differently. These are not usually manufactured but are usually plant material, and a few come from insects or shellfish. They are our original way of colouring textiles, substances that have a long tradition of use. Every climate has different plants found to contain dyes that can be applied to fibres. Now, they can be bought from specialist suppliers in the form of dried plants, or seeds of dye plants to grow yourself. Contact your local group or supplier for more information: in the UK, the Association of Guilds of Weavers, Spinners and Dyers (with a branch in each county) run classes or workshops on working with dyes.

The process is not straightforward, as colour from dye plants is not usually readily accessible to the yarn. In other words, the dye does not simply flow out into the yarn but has to be made available, which involves soaking the yarn

*Some basic equipment used for dyeing a skein of wool in acid dyes that are brought to the boil and fixed with vinegar.*

with a mordant prior to dyeing. The general name 'natural dye' is a bit misleading as the mordants are chemicals, but no dye method is possible without chemicals of some kind. The process of using these dyes can be hugely exciting, partly because the results are not always predictable, but also because if you use different mordants, you will get different colours from the same dye source, all in the same dye bath. Yarns treated with different mordants can be put together in one dye pot, and varying shades emerge: brighter shades from some mordants, duller from others – it's magical to see. The colours obtained are gentle rather than brash, but can still be strong and intense. Look at paintings from before the nineteenth century to see the rich and subtle colours in people's clothes: Tudor silks, moss-green velvets, madder reds, or Gainsborough's sky blue silks – all from natural dyes. Perhaps the most famous plant dye is indigo, giving a range of shades of a warm blue, known best as the true blue denim colour. It is manufactured now, but the dye is

*Dipping part of the skein in the dye for a space-dyed effect.*

*Dip-dyed yarn.*

contained in the plant Indigofera tinctoria, which grows in many countries with a warm climate. In Britain we obtained the same dye, although in a weaker form, from woad. This particular blue has the quality of being as beautiful as it fades as it is at full strength: it keeps the blue shade as it ages and bleaches without dulling or turning grey.

Natural dye colours also seem to have a natural affinity to each other; they are not scientifically 'pure' colours, but have a softness that makes them relate to each other. The strength of colour can vary and again can be unpredictable, depending on the age of the plant material, the weather and growing conditions as well as hardness or softness of water and many other factors, so they are more difficult to match and repeat than 'chemical' dyes. You have to decide which method suits you best and whether repeating colours accurately is important to you, or immaterial.

## Special effects in dyeing

### Patchy colours

If you use a straightforward method for dyeing wool according to your instructions, and stir it gently during the dyeing process, the colour will be evenly spread over the yarn. Conversely, if you want an uneven, patchy effect, the opposite applies: don't stir it! Don't dissolve the dye thoroughly first: sprinkle the powder onto the yarn, and don't move the yarn around, and it will settle interestingly in patches of strong and weak colour. If several colours are involved, they will also show separately in patches. The results will be random, but there are also ways to control your random patchiness. The attraction of patchy yarn is the way it knits; the patches disperse to arrive in different patterns and to give a soft, worn, varied effect.

A simple way to get more defined patches of colour is to 'dip dye' by hanging the hank of yarn over a stick or stirrer laid across the dye pot, so only part of the hank is submerged in the dye. This will give you dyed and undyed patches. For two different colours on one yarn, use two dye pots alongside each other and drape the hank across so that it dips in both. The central area will not reach the dye, and you may need to fill the containers quite high with liquid to get as much coloured area as possible. If you are left with unwanted white patches, you could repeat the process dipping the white areas in the dye with the same or different colours. In this way you get two colours plus white in one dyeing, or four colours in two dyeing sessions. This works well with two neighbouring

*Dip-dyed (left) and tie-dyed (right) yarn.*

*Preparing a skein for tie-dyeing, tying thick string tightly to prevent the dye entering the yarn.*

electric rings or burners on a hob: if your dye pans are the right size, and your skein or hank long enough, use more pots to obtain more colours on your skein.

### Tie-dyeing

Another way of patterning yarn is to tie-dye it. As on fabric, the idea is to tie the yarn tightly enough to prevent the dye penetrating the yarn. This can be done with strong string, or with something more water-resistant like polythene, but it is the tightness of the tying as much as the material used that gets the result.

Lots of small ties will produce white dots or flecks on your yarn. If you want to dye enough yarn to make an even speckle pattern on several hanks so that the effect is evenly spread over a piece of knitting, the hanks need to be the same size and tied in the same pattern. A skein-winder helps with this as you can use the struts on the winder as a guide to make your ties at set intervals.

This method of pattern-making is used in traditional 'ikat' weaving in some Middle Eastern and Far Eastern countries, making geometric patterns that blur slightly as the threads move during the weaving; but knitting works differently. It is much easier to predict and make a planned pattern in weaving than in knitting, as the tying is done after the warp is made ready to go on the loom. Knitting is not so easy to plan for as the yarn travels in loops rather than lying straight, and it is difficult to know accurately how much yarn will be taken in each row, especially in hand knitting where the tension might also vary. However, it is possible to make definite patterns, as is evident with the commercially space-dyed yarns available for knitting socks where the colour is applied in patches that make small patterns imitating Fair Isle knitting. If you want to plan this yourself, you need to do an experimental row of knitting or two, undo the knitting and measure how much yarn was used, and make your tie-dyed pattern accordingly.

*Space- or dip-dyed yarn in rust, blue and white shows up differently in different stitches.*

*In modular knitting, the colours are concentrated into patches.*

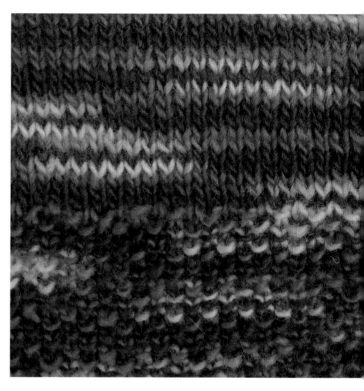

*Over an area of plain or textured knitting, it appears streaky and random, but the pattern will change according to the length of the rows.*

*Entrelac knitting: again the colours form blocks or patches.*

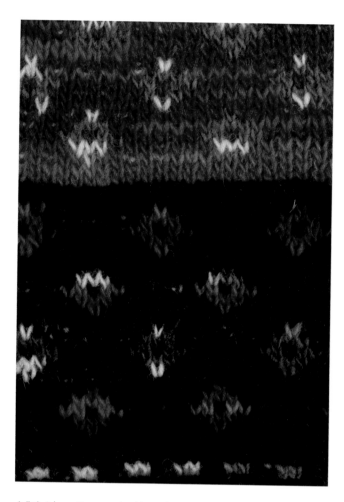

*A Fair Isle pattern worked in a plain yarn with a space-dyed yarn forming the motifs. This breaks up the streakiness and enlivens a regular pattern.*

*Short rows worked like the 'short-row circle' in Chapter 2, but forming a long curvy shape instead, the shaping emphasized by the random striping of the wool.*

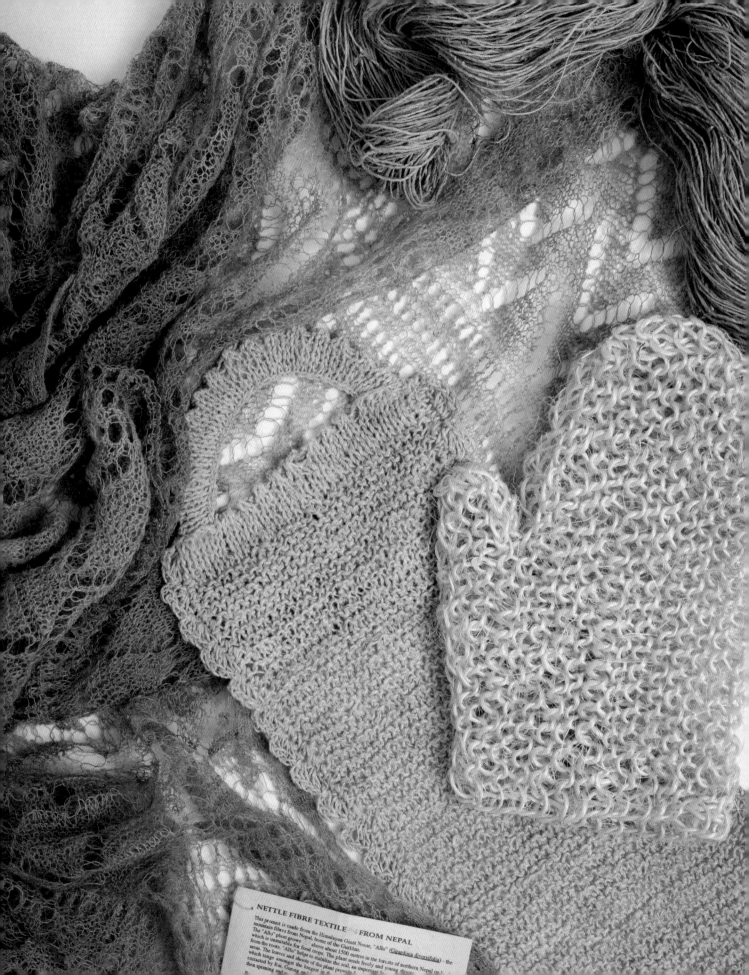

NETTLE FIBRE TEXTILE — FROM NEPAL

This product is made from the Himalayan Giant Nettle, "Allo" — contain fibres from Nepal, home of the Gurkhas.

The "Allo" plant grows above about 1500 metres in the forests of northern Nepal or h which is unsuitable for food crops. The plant needs freely and young shoots from the roots. "Allo" helps to stabilize the soil, an important for areas. The leaves and shoots of the plant provide f

which range amongst the longest in th

extracted by Rai, Gurung an

then spinning and

# CHAPTER 5

# MATERIALS

The best periods of Knitting have always occurred when yarns have been scarce or expensive,
as the desire for better knowledge of the work is stimulated in order that yarn need not be
unduly wasted.

Mary Thomas, *Mary Thomas's Book of Knitting Patterns* (1943)

This book has looked at how stitches can change the knitted fabric dramatically by being used in different combinations of knit and purl, with some slipping, increasing and decreasing. Going back a step further to the materials used in knitting, we can look at how different yarns behave and how they react to stitches differently. As we saw in Chapter 2, using the same yarn but changing the stitches can make fabrics that vary to extremes. Some knitted stitches can look woven or machine knitted, or even crocheted or knotted rather than produced by working in rows on knitting needles, but we can change our resulting fabric even more. Yarns are a more immediate and accessible way of changing the character of fabric we want to produce rather than just using different stitches.

Choosing fine and light or thick and heavy yarns is the easiest and most obvious way to alter the weight of the knitted fabric. There are so many exciting yarns available now that it is hardly necessary to find stitches to create warm or cool fabrics, as it once was when yarns were more uniform. Looking at knitting books from the beginning of the twentieth century, although knitting wools were available in a few different thicknesses, there was very little choice available. The only

'fancy' yarn was probably bouclé wool, so using stitches in a functional way was useful; for example, stitches to make warm fabric such as cabling, fisherman's rib, slip stitches or any that pull the knitted fabric inwards or upwards to make it thicker. Now we don't even need to know how to do Fair Isle knitting to make coloured patterns; multicoloured patterned yarns are available to do it for us. Textured yarns have become even more exciting and extreme, varying dramatically not only in thickness, but also in decorative texture, sometimes shiny, fluffy, silky, or spun with sequins, beads or a velvety texture.

It could be argued that all you need to do is to knit plain stitches to obtain a rich, varied result. Choosing different yarns is immediate and accessible whereas exploring and understanding knitted structure needs more time and effort. The aim of this book has been to examine everything about knitting, seeing how to use stitches creatively, as stitches need to be tried and experimented with if you are to understand their potential and to develop new ideas in knitting.

However, there is a world to explore in the underlying character of different yarns beyond the obvious visual decorative and thickness properties, even if they are plain and smooth, and not enticingly dyed in patterns, or spun into exciting textures. To go back to the basics, there are two main elements that influence the character of the final yarn: firstly the fibre, and secondly the way it is spun.

*OPPOSITE PAGE:*
*Knitted items in vegetable fibres: allo (Nepalese nettle), hemp and sisal.*

# Fibres

The different natural fibres used for spinning yarn have totally different characters and come from very different sources.

'Natural' fibres can be divided into two main families, animal and vegetable. Usually, animal fibres are spun from hair, fur or wool, and vegetable fibres from plant fibres, often fibres from the stem of plants (bast fibres), and sometimes from the fluff produced around the seed, as in cotton. There is a chemical difference between animal- and plant-derived fibre, which may help to explain some of the differences in the way they behave when knitted, and the way they take dye: animal fibres are made of proteins, and vegetable or plant fibres are made of cellulose.

## Animal Fibres

The best-known animal fibre is wool from sheep, but other animals are commonly used for their coats including alpaca and llama, the cashmere goat, and the angora goat which produces mohair. Less commonly, the coat of the angora rabbit, and also the undercoat from the quiviut and American bison are sometimes used, but in fact any hair or wool that can be spun into a thread with the strength to hold itself together could be used. Some animals, such as sheep, produce their fleece in such a way that it can be shorn annually; others are plucked or combed to extract the fibre.

Wool is different from hair as it has very fine scales on the surface, visible through a microscope, which help the fibres cling together and have more strength, whereas hair is smooth and therefore more slippery.

### Sheep

Different varieties of sheep have been bred over many hundreds of years, the older breeds having different types of wool suited to their original environment. Mountain breeds have tougher, thicker wool, often quite coarse, whereas downland sheep may have softer or silkier fleece. The softest and finest is from the merino sheep, originally brought into Spain from North Africa. Although the wool feels wonderful, it needs gentle handling when washing or dyeing as it felts very easily (and is consequently one of the best fibres to use for feltmaking). Contrastingly, wool from mountain breeds such

*Naturally coloured alpaca yarns, natural grey and black wool, handspun white wool and a cone of guanaco yarn.*

as Herdwick and Swaledale is much tougher and coarser, often containing rough hairs in amongst the wool fibres. Their wool is ideal for hard-wearing, tweedy fabrics. Other breeds have different characteristics, such as the lustrous, silky qualities of the Leicester breed.

Although most sheep are bred for white wool, which is a good basis for dyeing colours, there are other natural colours of fleece, often obtainable from specialist suppliers or small spinners. Best known are perhaps the Black Welsh Mountain sheep with a wonderful browny-black coloured fleece. Other breeds such as Shetland sheep produce shades of softer browns and greys, and natural grey wool is also spun from a blend of black and white. One of the attractions of these natural-coloured wools is their softness and natural sympathy with human colouring: like our own grey hair, there is not one flat colour in the natural wool, but varying shades which make a gentler, more mysterious colour than a dyed, flat grey or brown. These natural colours seem to compliment our skin tones and look harmonious in clothing. They are also a great foil for using in combination with brighter, dyed colours.

Natural wool spun from the fleece and without any other treatment also has a wonderful life of its own, with more character than wool that has been treated by scouring, dyeing and chemicals to make it machine washable. These processes can take away some of the bounce and natural spring in the yarn and produce something a bit flat and lifeless. It is possible to find natural yarn from small suppliers, and it is interesting to experiment with and feel the difference.

## Camelids

The camel family includes alpaca, vicuña, llama and guanaco. Although each breed produces wool with different characteristics, as a group their wool is quite different from sheep's wool, having a heavier, smoother, limper quality compared with the livelier, bouncier feel of sheep's wool. This is a generalization, as there are many variations in all these types of wool and in different parts of each fleece, and they can be changed again by the way they are spun; but there is an overall difference between, for instance, alpaca yarn and sheep's wool, and it can be wonderful for lace knitting, or for any garment needing a silky, heavy drape.

## Goats

Goats from different parts of the world produce cashmere, angora and mohair, again each having its own character and speciality. The natural fluffy nature of mohair has been enormously popular at different times, leading fashions for light, loosely knitted fluffy jumpers, but mohair can also be used in a sleek, shiny, smooth-spun yarn for suiting fabric: again, the spinning can change the fibre into something with a specific character.

*Cone of natural silk 'noile' which is short-fibred and matt-textured, and other more shiny silks randomly dyed.*

All the above animals are used for their fleece or wool on a commercial scale, but other animal fibres such as angora rabbit and dog hair are used domestically in hand-spinning, sometimes in different combinations and mixtures, or combined with wool to give more strength. Local spinning groups may be able to provide interesting and unusual yarns to try – *see* Further Information.

## Silk

Silk is also a protein fibre derived from an animal, but in this case produced by an insect, being the thread spun by the caterpillar of the silk moth. It is one of the oldest fibres used by man, and the best quality does not need us to spin it as the animal has done that for us. The fine filament is drawn off the cocoon in a continuous thread, then as the original thread can be extremely fine, it is twisted or plied with others to make a thread of manageable thickness.

The best-quality silk is reeled straight from the cocoon, but broken cocoons (where the moth has already hatched) can also be used to create more textured thread, spinning the broken fibres in a similar way to wool. Although this kind of silk thread is not considered the best quality, it has its own character, and broadens the scope of silk yarns available. There are many names for the different kinds of natural silk yarn: tussah silk has a natural creamy colour, and comes from wild moths. For a more knobbly, porridgey yarn, silk 'noile' is spun from broken cocoons; this has a rather flat, matt texture, but still the wonderful slightly crunchy feel of silk.

## Plant Fibres

Plant fibres are completely different in feel, look and quality, and the way they behave in knitting. Their use would have pre-dated animal fibres, being accessible to nomadic people before animals were domesticated. Many plants could be used in their natural state without preparation, such as vines, grasses and rushes for making cords, for weaving baskets, and for tying and joining. It is a small step to split the plant into finer strips, and to develop knotting, netting weaving and other constructive textile techniques.

Everywhere plants grow, in cold or warm parts of the world, they have been used in their natural state, especially in basket-making, and processed for making thread, with different methods involved according to how the fibre is extracted. Some plants need more preparation than others, and some fibres are more versatile and successful, resulting in large-scale farming. The plants listed below produce the better-known plant fibres.

## Cotton

Cotton needs a tropical climate to grow, and is found in Asia and is also cultivated in America. The part of the cotton plant (Gossypium) used for fibre is the fluff surrounding the seed, which has to be separated out so that the resulting thread is clean. The process of extracting the seed is known as 'ginning'. Usually the fibre is also bleached, although the trend for organically grown materials and a more natural look means that we are commonly seeing more of the natural, creamy-coloured cotton as well as bleached white.

There are different varieties of the cotton plant, and different qualities of fibre, and again various ways of spinning and treating the fibre and the yarn to produce different characteristics. Terms such as 'pima' cotton and 'Egyptian' cotton denote a particularly high quality and character, referring to the variety of the cotton plant, whereas 'mercerised' cotton has undergone a particular treatment which alters the chemical structure of the fibre, making it more lustrous and easier to dye.

Cotton is a cool fibre to wear, it can be fine or heavy, and does not have a particularly noticeable 'drape', although it naturally creases and is often treated or coated to counteract this tendency.

## Bast fibres

Linen, hemp, ramie and jute are described as 'bast' fibres. These are obtained from the stems of the plants, and are usually made accessible by a process of 'retting', which rots away the parts of the plant surrounding the fibre, allowing it to be extracted.

## Linen

Linen thread is obtained from the flax plant, Linum, which also gives us linseed and oil. As it grows in cooler climates, it is the natural fibre used in northern Europe for fine cloth and bedlinen, and to make a cool fabric (as opposed to the other native local fibre, wool). Linen was used in the UK and Europe before cotton was imported from India and the Far East. Although linen is also inclined to crease, it has several attractive characteristics, with a particularly good drape and weight.

*Lace knitting from Nepal in 'nettle' fibre, with natural and dyed hemp, linen and cotton.*

*Knitted pieces using cottons, and some linen and cotton mixes.*

## Hemp

*Cannabis sativa*, the industrial hemp plant, is used for fibre that can be very strong and hardwearing. Growing hemp does not require pesticides and herbicides, consequently providing a sustainable and environmentally beneficial crop with the end products ranging from fibre and food to fuel.

Traditionally used in the rope industry, as it is one of nature's longest fibres, it is very strong and hard-wearing. When spun finely, the thread is similar to linen and historically it is difficult to differentiate between them. It is harsh and crisp in its raw state, but with use and washing it develops an attractive drape, with a natural sheen.

The following plant fibres are less well known and not used much in knitting, but are better known for woven cloth, string or rope.

## Ramie

Ramie comes from the Boehmeria family, and is a nettle-like plant. It has a long tradition in fibre production and is used for clothing. It has some characteristics similar to linen and hemp.

## Jute

Jute is a coarser fibre from the Colchorus family, used mostly for string and rope, and famously for hessian, a coarse woven fabric used for sacks.

## Sisal

This comes from an agave plant (*Agave sisilana*), and we know it best when spun into string. Although sisal is not marketed as a knitting yarn, knitted pieces in sisal can be found in pharmacy or 'beauty' shops, sold as body-scouring mittens or strips for washing with.

## Bamboo and Soya

Recently, fibres have been manufactured from both these plants, but rather than using the natural growth of the fibre within the plant as in linen, hemp and the others, the plant material is processed and then spun into a manufactured yarn.

## Man-made fibres

Artificial fibres were developed in the beginning to imitate natural fibres, but then to improve and move forward in new directions, with qualities such as non-creasing and easy washing becoming more important to fit in with contemporary life. The range of yarns available is developing all the time, with an enormous choice of fancy yarns, patterned dyed yarns and yarns with added elasticity.

The more knitting you do, the more you become aware of the character of different yarns and fibres, and the descriptions above aim to help increase awareness so that you get to know by the feel and look of a yarn how it might knit up, and can choose the appropriate yarn for each project. Apart from how a particular yarn knits, how it takes the shape of the stitches, and how it drapes, the other considerations are how it wears, how long its life as a garment is, and how it looks and feels as it ages. The best yarns age beautifully in the way that wood, stone or brick look more beautiful as they get older. It all depends what you are looking for and how your knitting is going to be used.

## Spinning

There are basically two methods of spinning wool resulting in two different types of yarn.

### Woollen spinning

Usually fleece from breeds of sheep with shorter fibres are used for woollen spinning. The wool is combed or carded to clean and align the fibres in preparation for spinning with the fibres travelling widthways around the 'rolag' (the thick column of wool produced by carding), so that when it is drawn out and spun into a finer thread, the circular direction of the fibres traps air within the thread. This is important for warmth, but also makes a bouncy, elastic thread.

### Worsted spinning

Worsted spinning, on the other hand, is a way of spinning longer-fibred fleece. The fibres are combed and laid lengthways, then drawn out and spun into a smooth, often lustrous yarn with less bounce and stretch than woollen-spun thread. This has been made famous with woven 'worsted' fabrics used traditionally for men's suiting, which illustrate the smooth, lustrous quality that this kind of yarn and spin produces. Commercial knitting yarns are usually worsted spun as both the method and longer fibres make a stronger yarn.

There are many variations within these two categories, but in both types of spinning the next stage is plying: two or more strands of yarn are plied together to give extra strength and durability to the thread. Usually the thread is spun in one direction, described as 'S' or 'Z' (the middle stroke of these letters indicates the direction of twist); the plying is done in the opposite direction to create a stable yarn that will stay smooth and regular without twisting up on itself or distorting when knitted, but still retain the strength which is given by the spin or twist.

*Handspinner's spindle and wool carders, wool prepared for spinning, and experiments with felting knitting.*

## The Effect of Spinning when Used in Knitting

The first purpose of spinning is to give strength to the fibres. This can be tested with any loose fibres: hair, fleece found caught on fencing, grasses, or commercial 'cotton wool'. Try pulling the fibres out until they break apart, then experiment with twisting the threads as you pull, and you will see how much stronger they become.

Threads can be spun lightly or more tightly according to how soft or how strong the resulting yarn needs to be. Other fibres or materials, such as rag, ribbon or short pieces of yarn, can be brought into the spinning process to create texture: in bouclé yarns, one strand is fed into the plying process more loosely so that it buckles and gathers within the yarn. Other yarns are created where short lengths of fibre or material are trapped in the thread, so that knitting produces a textured soft-pile fabric. However, the basic aim in spinning a plain yarn is to obtain a balanced, level yarn that will stay constant, hold its spin without untwisting, and yet not twist up so much that it springs into coils and becomes difficult to use. The intention in a successful knitting yarn is that it will take the shape of the knitted stitch without fighting against it, bending or twisting, or influencing the stitch in any way that prevents it from being a normal, regular stitch.

So what happens if we try knitting with yarns that break the rules? An underspun yarn may be too soft, and come apart in the action of knitting: yarn does need a certain amount of strength and resilience to be manipulated over the knitting needles. On the other hand, an overspun yarn can have the effect of pushing the stitches in a particular direction, forcing them sideways, so that the knitted fabric is pushed

*Shropshire wool, singles spun S-twist: twist factor 2.75, turns per inch 4.75.*
*Top: Vertical columns of knit-side and purl-side stocking stitch, 10 sts each, washed after knitting.*
*Bottom: Bands of knit-side and purl-side stocking stitch alternating horizontally, twelve rows each.*

*Kent fleece, single spun S-twist: twist factor 4, turns per inch 6.98. LEFT: Vertical columns of knit-side and purl-side stocking stitch, 8 sts each. RIGHT: Bands of knit-side and purl-side stocking stitch alternating horizontally, 10 rows each. Samples have been washed after knitting.*

diagonally and will not lie square. Here is an opportunity for playing, and using the spin to shape the fabric without having to increase, decrease or use any knitting stitches other than knit and purl.

Overspun yarn is visibly lively, wanting to buckle under the pressure of the twist, so is not always easy to work with. In order to see the full effect of the twisting in the knitting, give it a light wash when finished, and it will react strongly and settle into the directional pull of the twist. If it is a single spun thread, not plied, the twist will act more strongly.

The simplest experiment is to work in blocks of knit-side stocking stitch contrasted with purl-side stocking stitch, either in vertical stripes or horizontal bands.

## Horizontal bands

If the spin is in the 'S' direction, the strength of the spin will push the stitches to the left, following the direction of the 'S' spin. So if you work a band of knit-side stocking stitch, then change to purl-side stocking stitch, the knit side will push the other way: still to the left when you look at the knit side, but changing sides and therefore making a zigzag fabric, travelling alternately to the left and right. In this case, the side edges zigzag.

## Vertical stripes

If the stitches are grouped In stripes of knit and purl, with perhaps eight stitches or more per stripe, again the fabric will zigzag, but this time the edges will be straight, and the bottom and top edges will zigzag up and down.

## S and Z twist

Supposing you can get hold of two yarns overspun in opposite directions, you can alternate the direction, as the 'Z' twist will lean to the right and the 'S' spin leans to the left. This makes it possible to work in all knit-side zigzag stocking stitch, changing from one twist to the other to make the zigzags; easy in horizontal bands, but more fiddly in vertical stripes as you would need to work with the two different yarns in each row, each in its own area in an intarsia method.

In all these experiments, you need to do several stitches or rows of each stitch to produce the effect. If you narrow it down to only two or even four rows of alternate knit and purl or S and Z, or two stitches vertically as in K2, P2 rib, there is no room for the stitches to react, the effects will cancel each other and it will look like ordinary knitting.

It may only be possible to find overspun yarn from a specialist spinner or a hand-spinner, but if you can, there is scope here for shaping fabric and therefore garments or other items in a different and interesting way that is very simple to construct.

*Yarn spun in different directions.*

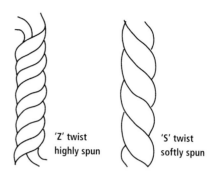

'Z' twist
highly spun

'S' twist
softly spun

*The same Kent fleece, knitted in stocking stitch, bands of S- and Z-twist alternating every 12 rows, washed after knitting. There is a lack of stability in single yarn, shown in the way the highly twisted yarn on the right has unspun on the corners of the knitted sample after washing.*

# CHAPTER 6

# Joining, finishing, edges and extras

Perfect knitting demands perfect make-up and it is here that so many are laggards and fall by the wayside. Many women will spend countless hours for weeks on end, knitting the pieces which are later to be made into a garment they have to wear, and they stitch those pieces together as though they were throw-out dusters from the rag bag. Careful attention to detail, using the right methods of seaming and finishing are the points which lend that 'extra' touch to home knitting and give it a professional status.

James Norbury, *Odham's Encyclopaedia of Knitting* (1956)

The tone of this quote gives us quite a jolt: evidently we have come some way in our attitudes since 1956. What is surprising is that James Norbury was not any man ignorant of the knitting tradition, but was in fact a knitting historian, knitting teacher and head designer for Patons.

Apart from the sexism of this remark, he has a point; it is certainly possible to ruin a garment by bad finishing. There is a huge choice of different ways of joining pieces of knitting together, from picking up with knitting needles or using a crochet hook, to sewing; and some are especially useful for particular purposes.

## Picked-up Joins

It is technically possible to knit most garments or other three-dimensional shapes in one piece without sewn seams by picking up stitches and knitting in different directions, but it might not always be practical. So we will look at picking up stitches first, and then at joining seams by sewing. Stitches can be picked up from any side or surface of the knitting to continue knitting in a different direction.

### Picking up from the bottom edge

Stitches can be picked up from the bottom edge, more easily from some cast-on edges than others (see below), and if the stitch also changes at this point (that is, ribbing picked up from stocking stitch), it helps to disguise any possible evidence of the join. You can always make a decorative feature by knitting two rows to make a dividing line or ridge, then beginning another stitch or pattern. It is useful to be able to lengthen garments in this way, to change the edge, or to leave the edging until last so you can see the garment and decide what you want.

For a perfectly invisible join, you could use a provisional cast-on, which leaves raw loops or stitches ready to pick up. It might be easier and more practical to change the stitch at this

*OPPOSITE:*
*Swatch for jacket to be picked up and knitted without seams.*
*a) Welting knitted sideways.*
*b) Body picked up and knitted with trellis pattern.*
*c) Sleeve picked up from the side, knitted downwards in textured pattern.*
*d) Frill picked up from bottom edge and knitted down.*

point. Working upside down means that your stitches have moved over by half a stitch; it would work in stocking stitch as this is the same either way up, but anything like ribbing or moss stitch would then move half a step and be out of line, as would a coloured pattern in Fair Isle.

## Picking up from the side edge

You need a good, strong, neat side edge to pick up from, ideally an edge where you have worked the first stitch of every row (whether knit or purl) and not slipped it. Slipping the first stitch of every row makes a neat finished edge, but is not as strong because the edge stitch has been stretched over two rows, so there is less substance to the fabric at the edges, and less firmness to pick up from. In a stitch like entrelac (*see* Chapter 2) where you are picking up one stitch every two rows along the side of the blocks it is ideal, but even then you can see that the join can look a bit holey if your knitting is not very firm.

Another problem with slipping the first stitch of each row is that it can cause tightness at the side, naturally shortening the edge, as there are in effect half as many rows on the edge as in the rest of the knitting. Altogether, slipping the first stitch is fine if this is the final, finished edge of a piece of knitting, but if the edge is to be joined any way, sewn or picked up, then work the first stitch every row.

Next, you need to work out how many stitches to pick up. In stocking stitch there are more rows than stitches to a given measurement, with about three stitches by four rows making a square. This is a rough guide, and worth checking on your own knitting tension, but in this case, if you are working entirely in stocking stitch, you could try picking up three stitches from every four rows of the knitted edge and it should lie flat. For garter stitch, picking up one stitch for every two rows works, as garter stitch pulls up lengthways. Ideally you need to assess what kind of stitch you are working in and check your tension.

Pick up the stitches from the very edge of the piece if it is strong and neat enough. If you pick up further in from the edge you will end up with a thick seam and it won't lie so flat.

If you are working the picked-up piece in a different stitch, then measure your tension in the new stitch, measure the edge to be picked up from, and work the calculation given in the sizing section in the introduction to the knitting patterns, Chapter 7.

There are times when you might also want to join your knitting to another piece along the side edge of the knitting by working it together as you go. If the other edge you want to join with is a top (rather than side) edge, this could be done by leaving the stitches on a stitch holder and knitting them together with stitches at the beginning or end of your rows (*see* example of knitting four squares, Chapter 2). To be successful, again the tension has to be right, and is different for different stitches. This can be calculated accurately following the guide in the introduction to the knitting patterns.

## Picking up from the surface

Stitches can be picked up from the surface of the knitting and worked in a different direction to make a textured sculptural surface, or to do something as practical as adding a pocket to a garment. It is simpler to pick up from purl stitches, especially if you are picking up along a horizontal row, as there are loops ready standing up on the surface rather than the smooth flat verticals in the knit side of stocking stitch. If you plan to pick up from the surface, you could put in a row of purl stitches to give you a basis to pick up from.

# Altering Length and Crochet Joins

If all your pieces of knitting are completed, there is another way to join them apart from sewing, by leaving stitches on a holder (or picking up a new row of stitches) and using a crochet hook to join them to the next piece (*see* 'crochet link join' below). This method is also useful if you want to lengthen or shorten a garment within the fabric rather than at the edge. For example, to alter the length, you might cut the welt off your garment, and either shorten it by taking out some of the length, or knitting up some extra length and rejoining the welt.

## Shortening the length

Cutting through a piece of knitting is easiest if there is a horizontal pattern, textured or coloured, so that you can see a row of knitting clearly. The edge of a coloured stripe is easy to see, and you can cut through alternate stitches on the purl side with a sharp-pointed pair of scissors, then gently ease the pieces apart. A row of purl on stocking stitch, or a change from the right to wrong side of stocking stitch would be just as easy to follow, again snipping

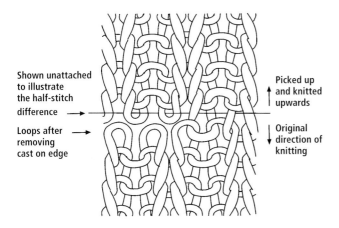

Ribbing steps half a stitch out when reversed

Shown unattached to illustrate the half-stitch difference →

Loops after removing cast on edge →

Picked up and knitted upwards ↑

Original direction of knitting ↓

*How stitches move half a stitch sideways if picked up from the bottom edge to knit downwards. This would not be appropriate for ribbing as it makes a distinct step out of line.*

alternate stitches and easing the pieces apart. If the piece is in stocking stitch with no patterning, it is difficult to follow the rows clearly, but you can pull a thread tight to make it easier to track, cutting as you go.

When you have cleaned up your edges, removing the snipped yarn, unravel (or cut out) the amount you need to shorten the knitting. It is not usually possible to unravel knitting from the bottom upwards: even stocking stitch, which looks the same either way up can lock at the ends of the rows and prevent unravelling, so you may need to cut again to remove a chunk of the knitting.

Next, put the stitches of each raw edge onto needles, preferably circular needles, as you can then spread out the knitting so you can it see clearly without the stitches being bunched together. The top edge of the knitting will be easier to pick up, as this is the way the stitches were travelling. Depending on the stitches used, the bottom edge may be more difficult as the loops are actually half-stitches, sometimes difficult to recognize. If, for instance, you were working in ribbing, the stitches would not look quite like either knit or purl, but some rather foreign hybrid stitch crossing from back to front, and front to back, so check you are picking up the right number of these loops.

In Fair Isle colour knitting the stitches can be even more difficult to recognize on this upside-down edge, and you need to pick up stitches from some places where the yarns change colour and look more like a strand of yarn than a stitch. Just make sure that the loops you choose as your new stitches

are strong enough to work. Sometimes twisting them makes them stronger, or working through two of these unformed stitches at a time.

## Lengthening the knitting

Again, cut the knitting apart, this time at a place where you can pick up the upwards-facing stitches and carry on knitting until it is the length you want. Then put both lots of stitches on needles as before, and you are ready to join the pieces. There are three ways of doing this:

(1) If you want an invisible join, graft the pieces together.

(2) Cast off both sets of stitches together with a crochet hook.

(3) Use a crochet hook to make a linking join.
    (*See* below for instructions to work these methods.)

## Sewn Seams

Sometimes it isn't possible to avoid sewing seams; it becomes so complicated to join by knitting that it's more trouble than it's worth. There are also times when it is not appropriate to knit in the round, so sewing is the only option of joining pieces. Two examples of this would be:

(1) Knitting a jumper with narrow stripes. Knitting in the round means working in a spiral, so there will be a small step when the colour changes at the end of a round. This is more noticeable in a thicker yarn than in a fine one. Knitting separate pieces for the back and front makes it possible to match the stripes precisely.

(2) Working a pattern in intarsia, where each colour travels across its own area. When this is worked in the round, the yarns will end up at the 'wrong' end of each area for the following round, so again it is more practical to work back and forth, making separate pieces joined by seams.

Another reason for not picking up stitches to make a seamless garment is the practicality of managing the weight of the knitting. By the time you get towards completing a seamless garment or three-dimensional piece, it may be large and heavier than you want to handle. It can sit on a worktop while you knit, or in your lap, but the whole piece has to be lifted, shifted and turned as you knit, and this is often reason enough for knitting in separate pieces and joining later.

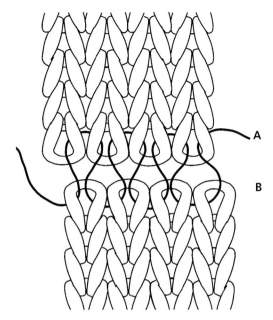

*Grafting knitting together invisibly.*

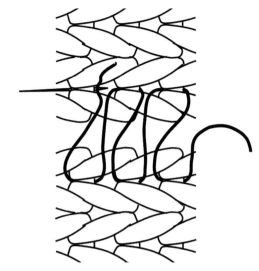

*A neat and strong method to sew a seam.*

## Invisible seaming or grafting

This is the best, strongest and neatest way of sewing knitted pieces together, and is done with a needle and length of yarn, preferably the same yarn used in the knitting.

When you join two pieces across the width of the knitting, that is top to top (as in a shoulder join), or top to bottom, you are following the direction of the knitted row: your sewn join imitates a row of knitting so that it becomes invisibly 'grafted'. This can be done to match stocking stitch on the knit or purl side, or a mixture of knit and purl stitches as in rib or moss stitch.

Using a length of yarn with a darning needle; the yarn has to travel through each knitted stitch twice. For example, for a stocking stitch join, put the stitches parallel as in the diagram and work from right to left:

(1) Pass the needle up through first loop A, down through first loop B.

(2) Up through second loop B, and down through first loop A.

(3) Up through second loop A, down through second loop B.

(4) Up through third loop B, down through second loop A, and continue in this way, following the diagram.

To imitate a purl stitch, reverse the 'ups' and 'downs' to bring the horizontal loop to the front.

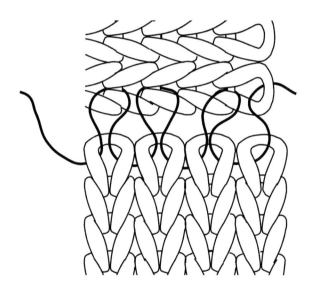

*Sewing side edge to top edge.*

## Seaming

If the pieces are to be joined along the side edges, or top edge to side edge, the process is still the same, with the row of joining again imitating a row of knitting: the needle and thread do not go just once through the edge of each piece in an over and over movement, nor in a sewn running stitch or back stitch, which would make a seam, but working in and out on one edge, then in and out on the other.

*Sewing a sleeve from stitches on a holder under the arm: see Pattern 6, Chapter 7.*

Rather than sewing into the side loop at the edge of the fabric, you go down and up (or up and down) through the horizontal bar that forms the top of the stitch; this bar is given extra strength by being inside the stitch rather than floating on the edge, and it makes an altogether firm but neat join. This kind of seaming is sometimes called 'mattress stitch', or 'ladder stitch', and is worked on the front, on the right side. It draws the edges together in an extraordinarily and satisfyingly invisible way.

One of the advantages of knitting is being able to join pieces right at the edge. Joining a piece of woven cloth in a conventional sewn seam means working on the wrong side of the fabric away from the edge to prevent fraying, leaving spare fabric forming a seam; but our knitting has a finished selvedge that won't fray, and therefore we can work close to the edge so that the join lies flat. The only condition to the join working successfully is that the edge needs to be good, strong and neat, not loose or loopy (*see* above on 'picking up from the side edge').

# Decorative Edges and Other Extras

## Cast-on edges with different uses

There are many ways to cast on. Some are stretchy, some firm, some decorative and some especially useful in different situations.

- **Knit-on cast-on** is the way most people first learn to knit, beginning with a slip knot on the left-hand needle.

  * Put right-hand needle into the stitch, make a new stitch, but instead of slipping it off, put the new stitch on the left-hand needle.
  Repeat from * until you have enough stitches.
  *It looks:* a bit loopy.

  *It feels:* stretchy.

  *Uses:* not the tidiest edge, but the loops are useful for picking up and knitting downwards.

  *Note:* you can knit into the back of the stitches on the first row to tighten the loops.

*Knit-on cast-on.*

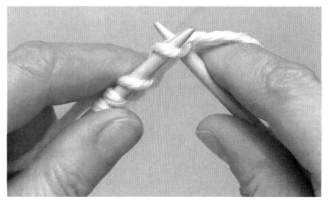

*Working the knit-on cast-on.*

Cable cast-on.

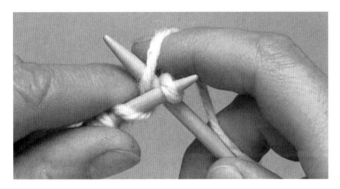

Working the cable cast-on.

- **Cable cast-on:** the same as knit-on cast-on, but knitting between the stitches on the left-hand needle instead of through each stitch.

  *It looks*: neat.

  *It feels*: firm, sometimes too firm.

  *Uses:* for a jacket edge or something that does not need much stretch.

- **Single thumb twist cast-on** uses a needle in the right hand only.

  (1) Make a slip loop on RH needle.

  (2) Twist yarn over L thumb by starting with the thumb above the yarn, and place on RH needle. Repeat until you have enough stitches.

  *It looks:* neat.

  *It feels:* stretchy.

  *Uses:* this edge is tight to knit on the following row but has the advantage of working along the RH needle in the same direction as the knitting, so is useful for buttonholes, or any time you need to cast on in the middle of a row.

- **Two-end thumb twist cast on:**

  (1) Make a slip knot some way along the yarn and put on the RH needle, leaving a tail end, which is used as in single thumb twist cast-on.

  (2) Insert the RH needle into the loop on the thumb and knit with the main yarn to make stitches.

  *It looks*: the same as the single thumb twist cast-on but with a row already knitted, so there is already a knit and purl side to it. If you are working in stocking stitch, purl the first row; then the smoother side becomes the knit side.

  *It feels:* very stretchy but firm.

  *Uses:* suitable for most edges.

  *Variation:* use a second colour instead of the 'tail' for a contrast edge.

To calculate how long a tail to leave, experiment by casting on 20 stitches, unravel them, and measure the tail. Multiply this up for the number of stitches you need.

Thumb twist cast-on.

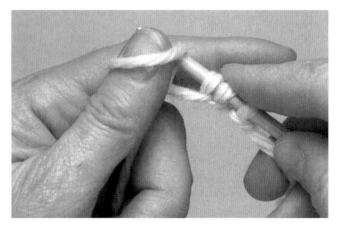

Working the thumb twist cast-on.

*Knotted edge cast-on.*

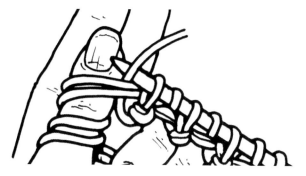

*Working the knotted edge cast on.*

- **Knotted edge cast-on** (Channel Island method): this is a similar method to thumb twist with two ends, needing a tail of yarn (or second yarn) but this time used double to make loops over the thumb (and in the other direction), and a main yarn for making stitches. Alternate stitches are knotted, with a plain 'yarn over needle' between each one. It produces a knotted edge, with the knots spaced out by the 'yarn overs'.

Make a slip loop on RH needle, some way along the thread, as the tail end is used double.

(1) Twist the doubled end twice round the L thumb, beginning with the thumb under the yarn (in opposite direction to thumb twist cast on), and knit through both loops to make a st on RH needle with the single (main) yarn, pulling double yarn through carefully until firm.

(2) Place single (main) yarn over RH needle (this makes a stitch).

Rep 1 and 2, so alternate sts have knots, with plain 'yarn overs' between.

*It looks:* decorative but firm, not dainty, with 'blips' or knots along the edge.

*It feels:* strong and stretchy.

*Uses:* It works best tightly knitted, with thicker yarn and a fine needle: the effect is lost with loose tension. The illustration is in chunky yarn for clarity. It could be used for any knitting where you don't want a straight ridge at the bottom edge.

*Variation:* Again, a contrast colour could be used for the knotted edge.

It is best used with a flat fabric: for instance this cast-on is used in the traditional guernsey sweater where five-ply wool is knitted on 2.25mm (US1/UK13) needles, followed by garter stitch.

- **Cast-off cast-on** uses a crochet hook to make the stitches around the knitting needle and has a variety of uses.

(1) Make a slip loop onto LH needle.

(2) Hold a crochet hook in your RH, insert hook into loop and put the yarn over the hook to make a st, keeping it on the hook.

(3) Now place crochet hook over needle, and pick up yarn, pulling through to make a st over the needle. (Leave the stitch formed on the crochet hook.)

(4) Pass yarn round so it is below needle again, and rep from 3.

*Crochet cast-on.*

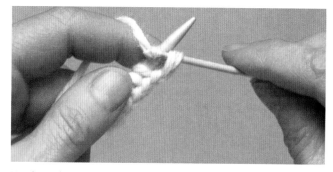

*Working the crochet cast-on.*

The last stitch is transferred from the crochet hook to the needle.

*It looks:* identical to a normal cast-off edge.

*It feels:* tight and firm, like a cast-off edge.

*Uses:* when cast-on and cast-off edges need to match: so, if working a jacket across sideways from cuff to cuff, use this cast-on and the cuffs and front edges will match.
It can be adapted for other uses, see below.

• **Provisional cast-on:** cast-off cast-on can be used as a provisional edge by working it in a smooth contrast yarn that is removed later. Instead of putting the last crochet loop on the needle, break the yarn off and pull the end through loosely, and take up your main yarn to begin knitting. The cast-on can then be unravelled later, leaving raw edge stitches to be picked up.

*Uses:* for picking up stitches and knitting in a different direction.

• **Invisible cast-on** (crochet hook): use cast-off cast-on to make an invisible edge for knit 1, purl 1 rib.

Cast on half the stitches you need by the above method. Knit 1 row, increasing after each st by wrapping yarn under, then up front of needle. [that is, a 'yarn over']. On the last stitch, knit into front and back of st.
**Row 1** * K1, yf, S1, yb, rep from * to end. NB. Slip all sts purlwise.
**Row 2** Your stitches should now look like knit and purl, so you can start the rib, knitting the 'yarn overs' and purling the stitches that were knitted in the first row.
After a few rows, remove the provisional cast-on edge.

*It looks:* as if there is no 'cast on' – the ribbing goes right round the bottom edge.

*Crochet 'provisional' cast-on for using with ribbing.*

*It feels:* stretchy.

*Uses:* for a professional-looking rib, or as a base for 'tubular' knitting.

• **Invisible cast-on** (for three-dimensional knitting, for example, a sock toe):

(1) Holding two double-ended needles parallel, and keeping a firm hold of the end of the yarn, wind your yarn in a figure-of-eight backwards and forwards around the two needles until you have enough stitches.

(2) Knit the stitches off the first needle, turn the two needles round and continue knitting off the second needle.

Once you have knitted all the way round, the original yarn end will be held in by the knitting.

This cast-on is used for beginning a sock from the toe up, with a smooth toe and no 'ridge' from the cast-on. To make a sock, you will need to increase at either end

*Invisible cast-on used for beginning socks at the toe.*

**Hold this end**

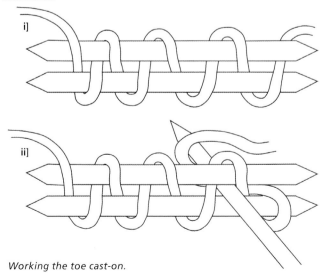

*Working the toe cast-on.*

of both needles until you have enough stitches for the circumference of the foot. You could also use this cast-on for double or tubular knitting.

- **Invisible cast-on for knit 1, purl 1 rib**: in effect, this is casting on alternate knit and purl stitches, as in rib.

Make a slip loop on LH needle, and cast on a second stitch.

(1) * Yarn to front, insert RH needle from the back to the front bet these 2 sts, take the yarn round the needle as if to purl, and draw the yarn through onto the RH needle, taking care not to twist it as it is placed on LH needle.

(2) Take yarn to the back, insert the RH needle from front to back bet the last 2 sts on LH needle, take the yarn round the needle as if to knit, and draw the yarn through onto the RH needle, taking care not to twist it as it is placed on LH needle.
Cont from * until you have enough stitches.

*For ribbing:* with an odd no of sts, begin the next row with a purl st; with an even no, begin with a knit stitch (the stitches should already look like knits and purls).

*It looks:* a tidy, professional-looking edge for ribbing, with no contrasting line at the bottom: the stitches grow from the very edge.

*It feels*: stretchy.

*Uses:* It also makes a good edge when knitting a double or tubular fabric, in which case you knit the knit stitches and slip the purl stitches.

*Casting on for ribbing.*

- **Picot-point cast-on:** this is made as a picot-point chain, picking up the stitches along the edge of the chain to form the basis of the knitting.

(1) Make a slip loop on LH needle.

(2) Use knit-on cast-on to make 2 more sts.

(3) Knit and cast off until 1 st left.

(4) Put st on RH needle back on LH needle, and rep from 2, until it is long enough to pick up the required no of sts.

(5) Using the remaining stitch as the first stitch, work along the picot strip and pick up 2 loops from each 'point', so cast on half as many points as stitches needed.

*It looks:* a decorative edge formed of a chain of little knots or 'blips'. If this is followed by a flat rather than gathered stitch, the edge shows more clearly: for example, moss or garter stitch. If 1 stitch were picked up from each point, the effect would be more gathered and frilly.

*It feels:* stretchy.

*Uses:* It has often been used in lace knitting, and would work well with an open, lacy stitch.

This stitch is best used with a flat or lacy stitch: a gathered stitch like ribbing will make the edge quite frilly.

The sample has been knitted in chunky wool for clarity: knitted finely, it makes a dainty edge.

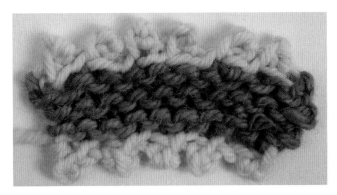

*Picot-point cast-on and cast-off.*

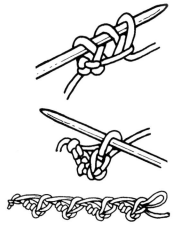

*Working the picot-point cast-on.*

## Casting off

There are not as many ways of casting off as casting on, because the action of casting off is to secure the stitches by linking them sideways over each other, which can only be done in two ways: right over left, or left over right.

- **Knit and cast off:** the stitches lie over each other from right to left.

  (1) Knit 2 sts.

  (2) Using the tip of the LH needle, lift the first st on RH needle over the last knitted st (that is, RH st over LH st).

  (3) Knit another st, and rep from 2.

  This is the most commonly used form of casting off, giving a neat chain edge with very little stretch.

- **Crochet cast-off:** a much quicker and more efficient method is to use a crochet hook instead of the RH needle, and work single crochet to cast off all the stitches (see crochet cast-off join below for more details). In fact, any crochet stitch could be used to cast off, as all crochet stitches produce a cast-off chain, so you could improvise at this point.

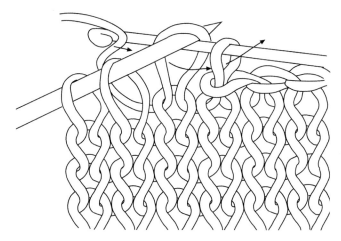

*Working the crochet cast-off.*

- **K2-tog cast-off:** although the loops are still laid over each other, they go from left to right in pairs, instead of from right to left in a chain, so the appearance is different, and there is no visible hard line, although there is no more stretch than in a normal cast-off edge.

  * K2 tog, place RH st onto LH needle, and rep from *.

*Two-end thumb twist cast-on, K2 tog cast-off.*

- **Crochet cast-off to join two pieces:** casting off both sets of stitches together is quick and easy and very strong, and makes a strong cast-off ridge rather than a flat join. If this is done on the wrong side, it won't be seen, but would still show on the right side as a less flexible ridge, unless the knitting is heavily textured.

  It is ideal for joining shoulders, as it is so strong and firm, and the 'ridge' produced can be used decoratively. It has been used traditionally for joining shoulders on guernseys and other fishermen's jerseys in the UK. The shoulders don't have to be a straight line, but could still be shaped by using short rows and keeping all the stitches on the needle until ready to cast off.

  (1) Put your two needles holding the stitches parallel, wrong sides together if you want the cast-off ridge to show on the right side (or the other way round for the seam to be on the wrong side), and hold them in your left hand.

  (2) With the crochet hook in your right hand, crochet through both the front and the back stitch, pulling the yarn through to make one stitch on the hook.

  (3) * Insert the hook through the next two stitches (first stitch on both needles), and pull the yarn through both stitches and then through the stitch on the hook, making a new stitch on the hook. *

  (4) Repeat from * to * until all stitches are cast off. Pull yarn through last stitch to fasten off.

  To make this join even more of a design statement, cast off in a contrast colour, or use a fancy cast-off such as 'picot' cast-off, see photos for picot point cast-off and frilled edge.

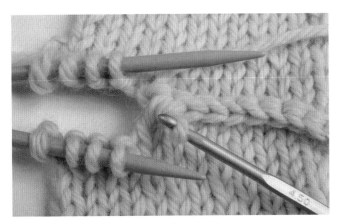

*Casting off 2 sets of stitches together*

*Crochet link join.*

- **Crochet link join:** in this join you don't work with any extra yarn, but simply pull the existing stitches through each other. It makes a flat join, unlike the crochet cast-off to join to pieces, but it is visible as a slightly zigzagging fine line. It has a lot more stretch than a cast-off edge, as it joins the stitches one by one instead of working through two at a time. This causes a slight zigzag as they do in fact make a wider row than the rest of the knitting.

It is a good, sound way to join flat pieces if you incorporate the line into the pattern as a feature, or use it as the boundary of a change of stitch or pattern.

(1) Put your two needles holding the stitches parallel, wrong sides together, and hold them in your left hand with the crochet hook in your right hand.

(2) Lift the first stitch from the back needle onto the hook.

(3) * Lift the first stitch from the front needle onto the hook and through the stitch on the hook.

(4) Lift the first stitch from the back needle onto the hook and through the stitch on the hook. *

(5) Repeat from * to * alternating front and back stitches until you get to the last stitch. Now use a short length of yarn to thread through the last stitch, and fasten, knot or sew in the ends neatly.

- **Picot cast-off:** this is the same method of making little raised knots as picot-point cast-on, but the knots can be spaced by a number of plain cast-offs in between. Apart from being a decorative edge, it has much more stretch than a plain cast-off, so works well for necks, cuffs and so on.

(1) Knit and cast off 3 sts.

(2) * Put last RH st back on LH needle, and work as for picot-point, cast on 2 and 3.

(3) Rep from (1).

## Other edgings

- **Frilled edge A** (from 'Bell Frill' in *Mary Thomas's Book of Knitting Patterns* (1943): this frill starts within the knitting from the widest part of the frill, decreasing to make the 'bell' shapes.

**Row 1** (Right side) Knit.

**Row 2** Using col A: * K5, cast on 9 *; rep from * to *, ending K5.

The cast-on sts can be either single thumb twist cast-on, which works in the same direction as the knitting, is very neat, but a bit tight to knit in the following row, or any other cast-on where you will need to turn the work to cast on to the left-hand needle, then turn back again to knit the 5 sts.

**Row 3** Change to col B, knit.

**Row 4** * K5, P9 *; rep from * to *, ending K5.

**Row 5** * P5, K2 tog, K5, S1, K1, psso *; rep from * to *, ending P5.

**Row 6** * K5, P7 *; rep from * to *, ending K5.

**Row 7** Using col C, * P5, K2 tog, K3, S1, K1, psso *; rep from * to *, ending P5.

**Row 8** * K5, P5 *; rep from * to *, ending K5.

**Row 9** * P5, K2 tog, K1, S1, K1, psso *; rep from * to *, ending P5.

**Row 10** * K5, P3 *; rep from * to *, ending K5.

**Row 11** Using col D, * P5, S1, K2 tog, psso *; rep from * to *, ending P5.

**Row 12** * K5, P1 *; rep from * to *, ending K5.

**Row 13** * P4, K2 tog *; rep from * to *, ending P5. Break off col B.

**Row 14** Using col A, cast off in K and P.

- **Frilled edge B:** this frill is worked the other way up, from the narrowest part, increasing to make the bells.

Begin frill with right side facing working on a multiple of 6 sts + 5 edge sts. This example increases every 4 rows to make a longer, more gradual frill, and is worked in stripes. To make the same size frill as frilled edge A, increase on alternate rows.

**Row 1** Knit.

**Row 2** * K5, P1 *; rep from * to * to last 5 sts, K5.

**Row 3** * P5, M1, K1, M1 *; rep from * to * to last 5 sts, P5 to end.

**Row 4** * K5, P3 *; rep from * to * to last 5 sts, K5 to end.

**Row 5** Change to col C, * P5, K3 *; rep from * to * to last 5 sts, P5 to end.

**Row 6** As row 4.

**Row 7** Increase again: * P5, M1, K3, M1 *; rep from * to * to last 5 sts, P5 to end.

*Frill used as a neckband (decreasing), at beginning of sleeve (increasing), and shoulders joined by picot cast-off.*

**Row 8** *K5, P5 *; rep from * to * to last 5 sts, K5 to end.

**Row 9** Change to col D, *P5, K5 *; rep from * to * to last 5 sts P5 to end.

**Row 10** As row 8.

Cont in this way, increasing either side of the knit sts every 4th row until you have K9, P5. Work one more wrong-side row, then to finish, using contrast colour, * P5, cast off 9 *; rep from * to * to last 5 sts, P5 to end.

Either of these frills can be worked with an open end, casting on or off at the widest part of the frill.

*I-cord, worked in chunky tie-dyed wool on 4 stitches.*

### • I-cord

*As a cord:* I-cord is a way of making a knitted cord on a double-ended needle. It is similar to a knitted cord made through a 'French knitting' doll, or a cotton reel with pegs in the top. It is in effect a tube of knitting and can be made on different numbers of stitches, but to knit an I-cord on needles, it works best with few stitches.

(1) Using double-ended (or circular) needles, cast on 3 sts.

(2) * Knit 3.

(3) Now either slide the stitches back to the other end of the needle without turning the needle and knit them again, or (if not using a double-ended needle) transfer them back to the left-hand needle and knit them again.

Repeat this process, always pulling the yarn firmly on the first stitch as it has to pull the stitches round into a tube.

*As a side edging:* to make a cord on the right-hand edge of the work using the 3 edge sts.

**Row 1** * K3, work to end of row, turn.

**Row 2** Work to last 3 sts, slip these sts, turn.

**Row 3** K3, pulling the yarn across behind the 3 edge sts. Slip them back to LH needle, and work again from *.

*NB* you are knitting the 3 edge sts twice instead of purling them on the wrong-side row.

**Warning:** the I-cord edging is in stocking stitch. If the rest of the knitting is in a stitch that pulls up, such as garter or moss stitch, you would need to do occasional extra rows of main knitting to prevent the I-cord from growing longer than the main fabric.

*I-cord used at the side and top of knitting.*

*As a top edging:* I-cord makes a neat cast-off edge, lying horizontally across the top of the knitting.

(1) At the beginning of the row (or if you are working in the round, starting where you want to begin casting off), cast on 2 extra sts into the first stitch using the knit-on cast-on method.

(2) * K2, S1, K1, psso (or SSK) (this uses the last st of the group of 3 + the next st).

(3) Transfer sts back onto LH needle.

(4) Rep from *.

(5) When you get to the last 3 sts, K2 tog, transfer the st back to the LH needle. K2 tog. Break off yarn and pull through. If you are working in the round, use the end to sew to the beginning of the cord to make an invisible join.

• **I-cord horizontally within the knitting:** this is a combination of the top-edge I-cord and Estonian 'braid' where one stitch travels across the row (miss out the first 'K1'). You can experiment with the number of travelling stitches for the cord: this is a 3-stitch cord.

*I-cord travelling across the knitting, marking the end of short-row segments to make the top of a hat. Stitches are picked up around edge, and I-cord worked followed by Fair Isle patterning, finishing with an I-cord cast-off at the bottom.*

(1) Knit to the position you want your cord.

(2) At the beginning of the row, cast on 2, * K1, S1, K1, psso.

(3) Slip 2 back onto the RH needle, yo, rep from *.

(4) At the end of the row, slip 2 sts back to RH needle, yo, K2 tog. Check you have ended up with the correct number of sts.

## Other Useful Extras

### Buttonholes

• **I-cord buttonhole (vertical):** make the I-cord up the side edge, working separately from the main piece for a short length to form a button loop or hole.

• **One-row buttonhole (horizontal):** this is a strong buttonhole, completed in 1 row. (Montse Stanley and Elizabeth Zimmerman have a similar one.)

(1) Work to the chosen position for buttonhole.

(2) Bring yarn to the front of work, and drop it.

(3) * Slip another st from LH needle to RH needle, pass first slip st over second to cast off first st. Rep from * until required no of sts are cast off.

(4) Slip last cast-off st back onto LH needle. Turn work.

(5) Pick up the hanging yarn and pass it between needles to the back. Using cable cast-on, cast on 1 more st than you cast off, but do not place last st on LH needle yet. Bring yarn back through to the front, between last 2 sts, put last st on needle. Turn work.

(6) Slip end st from LH needle to RH needle, then cast off extra cast-on st over it. Work to next buttonhole position and repeat the process.

### Tubular or double knitting

This is a way of knitting a double cloth or double layer of knitting on two needles, without working in the round, knitting and slipping alternate stitches to make the front and back fabrics. This sample is worked in two colours, which makes it easier to see the separate sides.

(1) Cast on the number of stitches for the width you want.

(2) Knit 1 row, increasing after each st by wrapping yarn under, then up in front of needle (that is, a 'yarn over'). On the last stitch, knit into front and back of stitch. *NB* the finished width will be half the stitches, the other half forming the double layer.

Continue as follows:

**Row 1** Using col A, * K1, yf, S1, yb; rep from * to end. NB Slip all sts purlwise.

**Row 2** Don't turn the knitting: knit again in the same direction starting the second colour (col B), * yb, S1, yf, P1; rep from * to end.

Turn work, crossing or linking yarns round each other to close the sides (otherwise you will have 2 separate pieces).

**Row 3** Using col B, as row 1, don't turn.

**Row 4** Using col A, as row 2.

Rep these 4 rows to produce a 'double' fabric, in a different colour each side.

*It looks:* when the 'provisional' cast-on thread is removed, it looks very like the 'toe cast-on', with stocking stitch travelling round the bottom of the knitting, but is worked on one needle instead of in the round.

*It feels:* stretchy, just like stocking stitch.

Uses: bags, hats, pockets or any double layer such as a scarf or tie that needs to hang flat.

It is also possible to form colour patterns, swapping the colours on the back and front, although this can then join the two layers.

## Preventing holes in short-row knitting

This technique is also described in the works of Montse Stanley.

(1) Before turning the work, take the yarn to the back.

(2) Slip the next stitch purlwise.

(3) Bring yarn to front, slip stitch back onto left-hand needle.

(4) Turn and work back, slipping first stitch purlwise.

*Buttonholes, using I-cord for a vertical hole at the edge, and a horizontal one-row buttonhole.*

*'Provisional' crochet cast-on being removed from knitting in 'double' cloth.*

# CHAPTER 7

# KNITTING PATTERNS

Every object is a record of a performance by its maker of a sequence of actions determined by conscious or unconscious decision: that is, it is evidence for the working practice, knowledge and skill of its maker.

Ruth Gilbert, textile historian, *Comments on analysing historic pieces of knitted fabric* (2010)

The aim of this book is to encourage understanding of how stitches work, and to promote experimentation. Following a pattern can be relaxing and reassuring with no thinking involved. It is (or should be) safe and comforting, and enormously satisfying. But why not improvise and make something individual?

The patterns included here are steps in a long evolution of knitting design ideas, both historically and in my own designing. No design comes without influences: we are all affected intentionally or unintentionally by what has come before us, and by fashions and ideas for colours and construction. Sometimes new trends or ideas seem to spring up independently in different places at the same time. Knitting is adaptable enough to follow trends, imitate patterns in embroidery or weaving, or to be used sculpturally and experimentally.

The following designs were sparked off by many different ideas. Firstly, exploring stitches and seeing what can be done with them to create textures and patterns. Secondly, playing with construction and aiming to knit in different directions with minimum seaming has been an interesting challenge. Occasionally there is a moment of eureka: 'if you do that then

*Detail of pattern 10 in a different colourway.*

*OPPOSITE PAGE: Details of Patterns 5, 3 and 7.*

this happens!' Lastly but most importantly, watching people trying on designs for thirty years has contributed enormously to designing for different people and different body shapes. The obvious way to shape a garment is to use increasing and decreasing, shaping the edges of each piece as in dressmaking and tailoring, but it is more fun and more of a challenge to do this through the use of stitches and construction.

An example of how a design can begin and evolve is the zigzag waistcoat. The lace patterns in Mary Thomas's knitting books got me thinking about shaping the fabric in waves or zigzags, which are traditionally small scale, and to try changing the scale so it dominates the design. I also wanted to make something stretchy, ribbed, and with interest on both sides of the fabric. The zigzags grew and changed, and the idea could be developed further.

Often my designs have evolved one from another, developing variations on a basic idea, changing the shape to become longer, shorter, more fitted, flared, loose, and so on. The modular patterns illustrate this, with the structure clearly visible. Modular knitting is a bit addictive, and its popularity is evident as it is used in many different ways. I was completely captivated when I first discovered it and realized the link with Elizabeth Zimmermann's mitred designs that work in a similar way.

These patterns show a natural evolution of a basic squares design developed into variations of shape, but also 'what if' became a big part of the process: what if the modules are not square? What happens if stitches producing longer or shorter fabrics are used, for example ribbing or welting?

The same goes for the 'entrelac' designs. The first time I saw this stitch was in a book of traditional stocking tops (*Designs for Knitting Kilt Hose and Knickerbocker Stockings* (1978) by Veronica Gainford), and then suddenly in the 1970s and 1980s it was popular with designers, and also seen in imported knitwear from South America. It has the extra fascination and bonus of producing a 'bias' or diagonal fabric that hangs and fits beautifully. But what if we change the stitch? It always seemed to be used with stocking stitch. What about ribbing, welting, or garter stitch?

These patterns are intended as jumping-off points to be improvised on, developed further, and made to suit individuals. They do not pretend to be fashion designs, but fashion always has an influence, affecting shaping of garments in the shifting emphasis on different parts of the body, sometimes without us being aware. Following the guides for working out shapes and sizing, these changes could be assimilated and adapted. Try different yarns, colours, stitches, and take them further.

# Guidelines for Using these Patterns

## Amount of yarn

The following patterns have been knitted in hand-dyed wool, designed and spun for me from Shropshire fleece by Diamond Fibres (*see* Further Information) unless stated (see the patterns in cotton or hemp).

This yarn knits up as four-ply, and any similar four-ply yarn can be used, as long as it knits to the same tension to produce the given sizes. (Or follow the guide below for working out your own size from a different yarn.) However, the weight and length of yarn should be taken as approximate. Different manufacturers produce 50g (1¾oz) balls of yarn, which may all be described as four-ply but have differing amounts of metreage/yardage, and different fibres also vary in weight and therefore length. Acrylics and other man-made fibres weigh less than wool, and cotton weighs more. If possible, always obtain more yarn than is listed and use any left over for other projects.

## Colours

The wool has been hand-dyed in acid dyes (in powder form) using a limited palette of red, blue, yellow, black, navy and brown (*see* Chapter 4). A wider range of shades is available from suppliers, but mixing these basic shades and altering the proportions gives an enormous range of possible colours.

The supplier will give precise directions for using and measuring the dyes, so the guides here refer to the proportions of each colour in grams per 100g (ounces per 3¼oz) of yarn. For example, red 1%, yellow 0.5% means 1g of acid red and 0.5g of acid yellow per 100g of yarn. (If using dye that comes in imperial weights, please follow the instructions from the manufacturer as to proportions to use.)

## Tension and sizing

*To work out sizing for 'modular' knitted designs*
You can use this method either to make a different size from the ones listed, or if your tension does not work out as described. It is also the way to work it out if you are using a different thickness of yarn than the one described in the instructions, so it gives you complete freedom to design your garment in your own size and in your own choice of yarn and needle size.

## Size

First, to work out what size you want to end up with, a good guide is to use a garment that you wear which is the size you want. This will give the right amount of 'fit' rather than working from your body measurement and trying to estimate how much extra to allow.

(1) Measure straight across a garment that is the correct fit for you, flat on a table.

(2) Go back to the knitting pattern and see how many squares or modules it has across the width. This works for the scallop-shaped and entrelac modules as well as for squares (*see* below).

## Measurement

If it is (for example) six modules wide, divide your measurement by six to find out how big each module needs to be. Be as accurate as possible, and don't worry if the size of each square is something fiddly like 11.75 or 8.33; a calculator will sort it out for you. If you are not accurate, this difference will be multiplied by six, so it will change the overall size. There is a simple calculation below to find how many stitches you need to cast on for each square.

## Tension

Try a square with the given number of stitches, but if the size comes out wrong, there are several ways of getting it right:

(1) trial and error: alter the needle size.

(2) trial and error: alter the number of stitches.

(3) the accurate way.

First, be sure you are happy with the needle size. If your knitting seems too loose or too tight, change to a smaller or larger size. This is worth experimenting with to get the feel you want, however impatient you feel; it could save hours of time later.

Knit a square in the smallest size stated in the pattern, for example 39 sts = 7.5cm (3in), and measure it from edge to edge. Measure it both ways and in different places, and take the average measurement.

Now go back to the size your square is supposed to be; for example 7.5cm (3in).

All the dyed wools are dyed using these six basic colours. The samples here are all 2% strength: acid navy, acid blue, acid brown, acid red, acid black and acid yellow.

## Formula for working out sizing

Using a calculator, work it out like this:

The measurement you want your square to be divided by the size your square has turned out, multiplied by the number of cast-on stitches in your square.

(NB. This calculation works for the full amount of stitches per module; it does not have to be the exact number of stitches in the measurement.)

So for example, if you want a 7.5cm (3in) square and your sample turned out 8.5cm (3¼in) having cast on 39 stitches, this is the calculation:

$\frac{7.5}{8.5} \times 39 = 34.4$ stitches ($\frac{3}{3.25} \times 39 = 35.9$ stitches)

so cast on 35 sts and it will produce a 7.5cm square. (You need an odd number of stitches.)

If your knitting is tighter and your sample was only 7cm (2¾in), the calculation would be:

$\frac{7.5}{7} \times 39 = 41.7$ stitches

so you need to cast on 41 sts to make it 7.5cm (3in) example 7.5 cm (3in).

### Entrelac

The same calculation will work, using the number of stitches in each module. Use the horizontal (diagonal) measurement across the module to give you the width as it will sit diagonally.

### Sizing any other stitch

The same formula can be used for working out any sizing or tension in any stitch: Fair Isle, cables, or whatever you want. It is also a useful method to work out how many stitches to pick up along the side of a piece of knitting.

- First, you need to knit a sample in the stitch you want to use, then measure the area you want to pick up stitches from, or the measurement you want to cast on ('a').
- Now measure your tension in the chosen stitch over a few centimetres (an inch) ('b').
- Count the number of stitches in this measurement ('c').

The measurement you want is now divided by the size of your test piece and multiplied by the number of stitches in this measurement. This gives you the number of stitches you need to pick up or cast on.

$$\frac{a}{b} \times c = \text{number of stitches needed}$$

### The patterns in this book

Following one of the modular patterns, even if you change the number of stitches in your modules, your yarn thickness or needle size, the knitting patterns in this book can still be followed for the way the design is constructed.

### Sleeves

For the sleeve tops, pick up a stitch for each stitch on the edge of the square, + 1 for the corner: that is, if your square has 45 sts, pick up 23 along edge of each module at the top of the sleeve.

### Larger sizes

As well as changing the number of stitches in each module, the other option for making a larger size would be to change the number of modules in the pattern, say 8 to the width instead of 6. This might be preferable: it depends on the balance and look of the design. The same calculation will work, once you have decided on the size of your basic module. It will be 'total width of garment divided by 8' instead of 6, then back to the calculation above to work out the number of stitches.

# Modular squares jacket

## Materials

4-ply wool, 25g (1oz) col A (82m), 25g (1oz) col B (82m), 100g (3¼oz) col C(325m), 350–500g (11½–18oz) col D 1,138–1,625m)

## Dyes

Col A: red 0.5%, yellow 2.5%, brown 0.5%
Col B: red 1%, yellow 0.2%, brown 0.1%
Col C: black 1%, brown 0.5%
Col D: blue 0.5%, navy 0.25%

## Needles

Size 3.25mm (US3:UK10), and 3mm (US2:UK11) needles for cuffs and front bands (a circular needle is useful for the top of the sleeve)

## Size

To fit bust 86[97:107:117]cm (34[38:42:46]in)

## Tension

Each square needs to measure 7.5[8.5:9.5:10.5]cm (3[3½:3¾:4¼]in). This allows for a comfortable fit, not too tight.

## Knitting level

Easy/moderate

*Pattern 1, colour codes.*

## Construction

This jacket is made up from squares that are linked as they are knitted. The squares are cast on (or picked up from previous squares) along 2 sides, and decreased in the centre on alternate rows to form the square shape, with the rows turning a right angle. They are knitted in garter stitch with a stocking stitch stripe and a colour change in the corner. The side seams are sewn at the end.

If you would like to avoid side seams, make 'double' squares to go round the sides and over the shoulders – see end of pattern for instructions, and Chapter 6 for illustration. *See* end of pattern for instructions, and diagram A for order of knitting the squares.

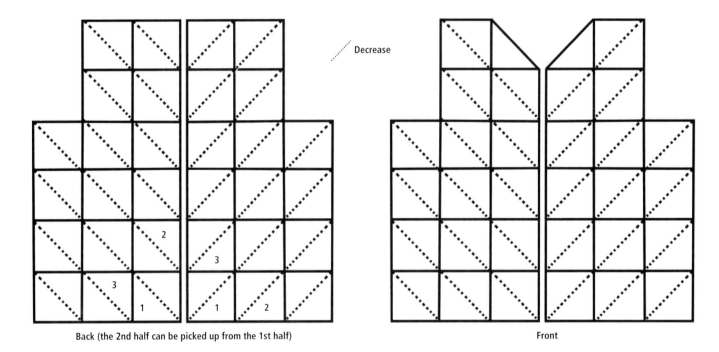

Back (the 2nd half can be picked up from the 1st half)　　　Front

*Pattern 1, diagram A: shape construction.*

## Square 1

This begins at centre bottom for each back and front piece, and the squares build upwards. See diagram A for the basic structure.

Using col D, cast on 39[45:49:55] sts.

* Knit back 1 row.

**Row 3** (right side) K18[21:23:26], S1, K2 tog, psso, K18[21:23:26]. Mark the centre with a tag of wool or stitch marker that can travel up the rows with the knitting to remind you where to decrease and keep the decreases in line: this sort of decrease makes a neat diagonal that is part of the design.

**Row 4** Knit.

**Row 5** K17[20:22:25], S1, K2 tog, psso, K17[20:22:25].

**Row 6** Knit.

**Row 7** Change to col C, K16[19:21:24], S1, K2 tog, psso, K16[19:21:24].

**Row 8** Using col C, *purl*.

**Row 9** Using col D, K15[18:20:23], S1, K2 tog, psso, K15[18:20:23].

Cont in this way, in garter st, decreasing on the centre 3 sts on right-side rows, until there are 9 sts left.

Change to col A, K3, S1, K2 tog, psso, K3. Continuing in col A, knit back.

Continue decreasing as before, until 3 sts left: S1, K2 tog, psso. Break off thread and pull thread through. * (Use A and B as corners on alternate squares.)

Weave the end in when picking up the sts for the next square, or sew in afterwards (*see* Chapter 4 for weaving in).

## Square 2

Using col D, cast on 20[23:25:28] sts, then with right side facing, pick up 19[22:24:27] sts along the side of Square 1: see diagram A. Repeat as for Square 1 from * to *.

## Square 3

Using col D, pick up 19[22:24:27] along side of Square 1: see diagram A. Then cast on 20[23:25:28] sts. Repeat as for Square 1 from * to *.

Now follow the diagram, and where the squares are between others, pick up all the sts from the previous edges.

Otherwise, cast on edges where needed.

Make a separate piece for each front, and 2 pieces for the back. NB the direction of the squares is different each half back and half front: see diagram A. You can pick up the sts for the second half of the back, or join by sewing at the end.

Make the shape as in the diagram, or adjust length with more or fewer rows of squares, leaving armhole as indicated, and shaping only for front neck.

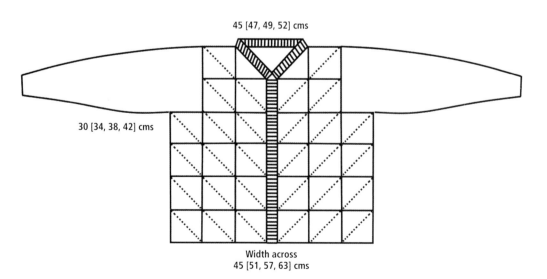

45 [47, 49, 52] cms

30 [34, 38, 42] cms

Width across
45 [51, 57, 63] cms

*Pattern 1, diagram B: measurements.*

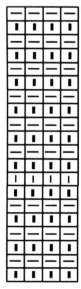

*Pattern 1 stitch chart.*

## Front neck shaping

(*See* diagram B for position of front neck triangles).
Work a triangle or half-square for front of neck by picking up
20[23:25:28] sts from side of one previous square, working in the
usual pattern straight across on these sts, decreasing 1 st at neck
edge corner on alt rows in place of the usual central decrease.

## Sleeves

(Worked from the top down)
Join the shoulders (*see* Chapter 6).
With right side of garment facing and col D, pick up the
stitches from the bottom of the armhole to the shoulder,
then down the other side to armhole, but not across
the underarm edge (*see* diagram B). Pick up and knit
20[23:25:28] sts per square (80[92:100:112] sts in total over
the 4 squares).

*Pattern:* * Work in garter st using col D, for 5cm (2in), then
change to col A. Work 4 rows stocking st, then rep from *, in
stripes of 5cm (2in) col D, 4 rows col A, B or C in any order.
When sleeve measures 24[26:28:30]cm (9½[10:11:12]
in), decrease 1 st at each end of next and every following
6th row. Continue until sleeve measures 45[47:49:52]cm
(17½[18½:19¼:20¾]in) or the length you want, and cast
off (in whichever colour you are using).

*Cuff:* If you would like a ribbed cuff, change to 3mm
(US2:UK11) needles, and knit one row decreasing to 60 sts.
Now work in K2, P2 rib for 3cm (1¼in) and cast off loosely.

## Neck and bands

*Neck:* Using size 3mm (US2:UK11) needles and col D, pick
up and knit 26[29:31:34] sts along slope of right front neck,
22[25:28:31] sts from each square at back of neck, and
26[29:31:34] more sts along left front neck. NB the ribbing
will pull in slightly, so 22[25:28:31] sts are needed rather
than the usual 20[23:25:28] sts. Work in K2, P2 rib for 8
rows, and cast off, not too tightly.

*Front bands:* Using col D, pick up and knit 22[25:28:31] sts
from each square, all along each front edge.
Work in K2, P2 rib.

*Buttonholes:* Place the buttonholes on the right-hand band level
with the top of each square, to fit the size of your buttons (*see*
Chapter 6). If you prefer, work a plain ribbed band and add
crochet loops afterwards. Rib for 8 rows altogether, and cast off.

## Finishing

Join side seams, sleeve seams and underarm seams, and sew
on buttons. *See* 'Finishing', Chapter 6, for sewn seams.
Alternatively, you could make this design with double
squares so there are no side seams.

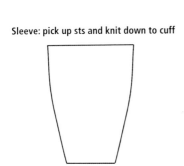

Sleeve: pick up sts and knit down to cuff

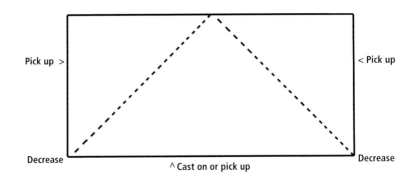

*Pattern 1, diagram C: double module.*

## Double squares

This design can be made without side seams and shoulder seams by fitting these double squares in at the sides and over the shoulders. You need to work each piece, front and back, from the centre towards the sides until you reach the position of the piece that will join the sides, then pick up the stitches from each half front and back to make the joining 'double' square. You need to double the stitches and follow the original instructions for each row twice.

Start with 78[90:98:110] sts, picked up as before from previous squares (39[45:49:55] sts from each square) or cast on where necessary. Knit back one row, then start pattern as before.

**Row 3** K18[21:23:26], S1, K2 tog, psso, K36[42:46:52], S1, K2 tog, psso, K18[21:23:26].

**Row 4** Knit.

**Row 5** K17[20:22:25], S1, K2 tog, psso, K34[40:44:50], S1, K2 tog, psso, K17[20:22:25].

**Row 6** Knit.

**Row 7** Change to col C, K16[19:21:24], S1, K2 tog, psso, K32[38:42:48], S1, K2 tog, psso, K16[19:21:24].

**Row 8** Using col C, purl.

**Row 9** Using col D, K15[18:20:23], S1, K2 tog, psso, K30[36:40:46], S1, K2 tog, psso, K15[18:20:23].

Cont in this way, in garter st, decreasing on right-side rows, changing col again when there are 18 sts left.

Using col A or B, K3, S1, K2 tog, psso, K6, S1, K2 tog, psso, K3. Continuing in col A or B, knit back.

Continue decreasing as before, until 6 sts left. S1, K2 tog, psso, S1, K2 tog, psso.

K2 tog, break thread and pull thread through.

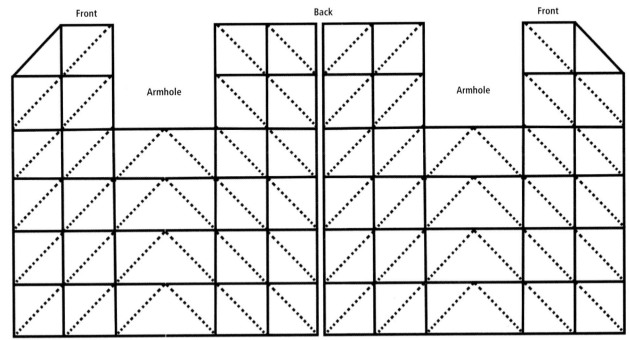

Double square at sides, no seams

*Pattern 1, shape construction.*

# Modular ribbed squares jacket

## Materials

4-ply wool, 50g (1¾oz) col A (163m), 375–500g (13¼–18oz) col B(1,220–1,625m), 100g (3½oz) col C (325m)

## Dyes

Col A: red 1%, yellow 0.2%, brown 0.5%
Col B: red 0.5%, yellow 2.5%, brown 0.5%
Col C: brown 0.1%, black 0.05%

## Needles

Size 3.25mm (US3:UK10) straight or circular needle(s) (a circular needle is useful for the top of the sleeve), and 3mm (US2:UK11) needles for neckband and front band

## Size

To fit bust 86[97:107:117]cm (34[38:42:46]in)

## Tension

It is difficult to measure tension in ribbing, but as a guide, the 43 st-sized module should measure 7.5cm (3in) without stretching (see sizing section at the beginning of this chapter).

## Knitting level

Moderate

## Construction

This jacket is made in the same way as the garter stitch modular squares jacket, but the 'squares' are knitted in K2, P2 rib, which will pull them into 'diamond' shapes (so they are called 'modules' in this pattern), and they make a heavily textured, stretchy and close-fitting garment.

The decrease used in this pattern will give a clear line running diagonally through the centre. See diagram for order of knitting the modules, and pattern 1 for the option of knitting without side seams.

## Module 1

This begins at centre bottom for each back and front piece. Cast on 43[47:53:57] sts in col C.

\* Knit back 1 row.

**Row 3** Change to col B, (right side) K2, P2 for 20[22:25:28] sts, S2 tog knitwise, (putting the needle through the stitches as if to knit them tog), K1, p2sso, rib 20[22:25:28], starting with P2 this time, so the ribbing is symmetrical and makes a neat pattern where it decreases. Mark the centre with a tag of wool or stitch marker that can travel up the rows with the knitting to remind you where to decrease and keep the decreases in line: this sort of decrease makes a neat diagonal that is part of the design.

**Row 4** Work in rib, purling the centre st, so that the decrease is always knitted on the right side and purled on the wrong side, making a neat line. \*

**Row 5** Rib19[21:24:27], S2 tog knitwise, K1, p2sso, rib 19[21:24:27].

**Row 6** Rib, purling centre st.

**Row 7** Rib 18[20:23:26], S2 tog knitwise, K1, p2sso, rib18[20:23:26].

Cont in this way, in ribbing, decreasing on right-side rows, ribbing and purling the centre stitch on wrong side rows. When there are 7 sts left, change to col A. Continue ribbing and decreasing as before, until 3 sts left: S2, K1, p2sso. Pull thread through.\*

If you are not getting the clear 'line' of the decrease, you may not be slipping the stitches in the way described.

Weave the end in when picking up the sts for the next module, or sew in afterwards.

## Module 2

Using col C, cast on 22[24:27:29] sts, then with right side facing, pick up 21[23:26:28] sts along the side of Module 1: see diagram. Follow instructions for Module 1 from \* to \*.

*Pattern 2, colour codes.*

*Pattern 2, stitch chart.*

## Module 3

Using col C, pick up 21[23:26:28] sts along side of Module 1: see diagram. Then cast on 22[24:27:29] sts. Follow instructions for Module 1 from * to *.

Now follow the diagram, and where the modules are between others, pick up all the sts from the previous edges. Otherwise, cast on edges where needed.

Make a separate piece for each front, and 2 pieces for the back, although the back pieces can be joined as you go, by picking up from the appropriate edge. NB the direction of the modules is different in each half back and half front: see diagram. This jacket is 4 modules long below the armholes. Leave armhole as indicated in the diagram, and work shaping modules for front neck.

## Front neck shaping

(*See* diagram for position of front neck module.)
Work a triangle or half-module for front of neck by picking up 21 sts from side of one previous module, working in the usual pattern, and decreasing 1 st at neck edge corner on alt rows in place of the usual central decrease.

## Sleeves (make 2)

These are worked separately from the top down. Join the shoulders (*see* Chapter 6).

With right side facing and col C, pick up the stitches from the bottom of the armhole to the shoulder, then down from other shoulder to armhole, but not across the underarm edge: see diagram. Pick up and knit 25[27:30:32] sts per module (100[108:120:128] sts over 4 modules) and knit back 1 row. Now change to col B, and knit 1 row, then work in K2, P2 rib. (Extra stitches are needed to give enough fullness to the sleeve top.)

*Sleeve pattern:* Work 4cm (1½in) rib in col B, then * change to col A or C (alternate stripes). On right side, knit 1 row, then purl 1 row. Change back to col B, knit 1 row (this makes a clean colour break), then K2, P2 rib for 4 cm (1½in). Rep from *.

*Shaping:* When you have worked 40cm (15½in), dec 1 st at each end of next and every following fourth row until there are 56[58:60:62] sts. When the sleeve measures 56[56:58:58]cm (22¼[22¼:22¾:22¾]in) (adjust the length here if necessary), cast off in whichever colour you are using.

## Neck and bands

*Neck:* Using size 3mm (US2:UK11) needles and col C, pick up and knit 26[28:31:33] sts along slope of right front neck, 22[24:27:29] sts from each module at back of neck, and 26[28:31:33] sts along left front neck. Knit back 1 row. Change to col B and work in K2, P2 rib for 6 rows, and cast off in rib in col C.

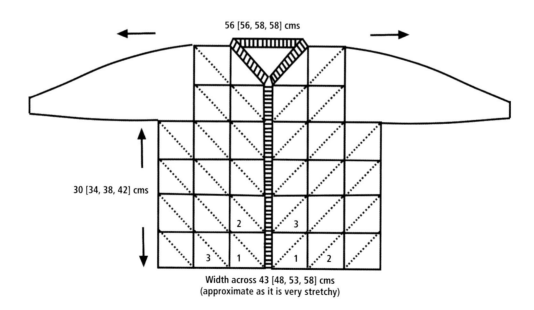

56 [56, 58, 58] cms

30 [34, 38, 42] cms

Width across 43 [48, 53, 58] cms
(approximate as it is very stretchy)

*Pattern 2, shape construction. The modules are shown square but will be distorted by the ribbing.*

*Front band:* Using size 3mm (US2:UK11) needles and col C, pick up and knit 26[28:31:33] sts from each module, all along each front edge. (NB again, extra stitches are required so the neck and front bands are not too tight.) Knit back 1 row in col C, change to col B and work in K2, P2 rib for 6 rows, making buttonholes on row 3.

*Buttonholes:* Make buttonholes on the right front band level with the top of each module (*see* Chapter 6). Alternatively, work a plain ribbed band and add crochet loops afterwards.
Rib for 3 rows, and make buttonholes on row 4.
Rib for 6 rows altogether, and cast off.

## Finishing

Join side seams, sleeve seams and underarm seams, and sew on buttons. *See* 'Finishing', Chapter 6, for sewn seams.

## Suggestions

*Pattern 2, another version in the same stitch, but with the modules knitted from the top down, dramatically changing the shape of the bottom edge.*

To make this garment without seams, see diagrams B and C, pattern 1, and follow the instructions above with double the number of stitches and decreases for the double modules.

If the modules are used upside down, the shape of the jacket will be quite different. Instead of the slightly scalloped shaping at the sides, the modules will point downwards at centre front and back. If you leave the centre back two modules unjoined, you will have a swallowtail at the centre back.

Follow the same instructions for each module, the sleeves and edges, but work from the centre top of the diagram downwards.

# 'Flares and squares' jacket

## Materials

4-ply wool, 100g (3½oz) col A (325m), 500–600g (18–21oz) col B (1,625–1,950m), 50g (1¾oz) col C (163m), 50g (1¾oz) col D (163m), 25g (1oz) col E (82m)

## Dyes

Col A: black 2%.
Col B: black 0.1%, yellow 0.5%
Col C: blue 0.05%
Col D: blue 0.5%, yellow 0.1% (unevenly dyed)
Col E: blue 2%, yellow 1%

## Needles

Size 3.25mm (US3:UK10), size 3mm (US2:UK11) for cuffs and bands, straight or circular (a circular needle is useful for the top of the sleeve)

## Size

To fit bust 86[97:107:117]cm (34[38:42:46]in).
Each square needs to measure 7.5 [8.5:9.5:10.5]cm (3[3¼:3¾:4¼]in).

## Tension

Each square needs to measure 7.5[8.5:9.5:10.5]cm (3[3½:3¾:4¼]in).

## Knitting level

Moderate. Modular knitting plus picking up and knitting in different directions, and short-row knitting.

## Construction

This jacket is made up from squares that are linked as they are knitted. The squares are cast on (or picked up from previous squares) along 2 sides, and decreased in the centre of alternate rows to form the square shape, with the rows turning a right angle. The squares are knitted in garter stitch, except for the stocking stitch stripe in rows 7 and 8.

The *flares* are knitted between rows of squares in garter stitch, picking up the sts and knitting 'sideways': *see* diagram A for order of knitting the squares and where the flares are inserted.

The pattern is written so that you make a separate piece for each front, and two pieces for the back. NB the direction of the squares is different for each half back and half front: *see* diagram A. You can pick up the sts for the second half of the back, or join by sewing at the end. Alternatively, you can make it without side seams: see 'double squares' at the end of the instructions.

## Square 1 – basic square (garter st with stripe)

This begins at centre bottom for each back and front piece.
Using col B, cast on 39[45:49:55] sts.
* Knit back 1 row.
**Row 3** (Right side) K18[21:23:26], S1, K2 tog, psso, K18[21:23:26]. Mark the centre with a tag of wool or stitch marker that can travel up the rows with the knitting to remind you where to decrease and keep the decreases in line: this decrease makes a neat diagonal that is part of the design.
**Row 4** Knit.
**Row 5** K17[20:22:25], S1, K2 tog, psso, K17[20:22:25].
**Row 6** Knit.
**Row 7** Change to col D or C (see main photo for colour order), K16[19:21:24], S1, K2 tog, psso, K16[19:21:24].
**Row 8** Using col D or C, *purl*.
**Row 9** Using col B, K15[18:20:23], S1, K2 tog, psso, K15[18:20:23].
Cont in this way, in garter st, decreasing on right-side rows on the centre 3 sts, changing to col E when you have 9 sts left. Using col E, K3, S1, K2 tog, psso, K3. Knit back. Continue decreasing as before, until 3 sts left. S1, K2 tog, psso. Break off thread and pull thread through. *
Weave the end in when picking up the sts for the next square, or sew in afterwards.
Follow diagram A to see when to pick up Square 2 or Square 3.

*Pattern 3, colour codes.*

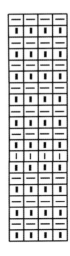

*Pattern 3, stitch chart. Garter stitch with stocking st stripe.*

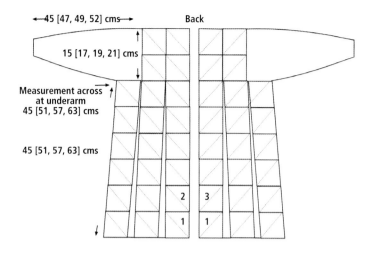

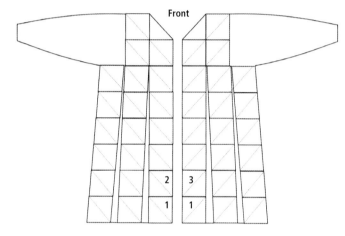

*Pattern 3, diagram A: shape and measurements.*

## Square 2

Using col B, cast on 20[23:25:28] sts, then with right side facing, pick up 19[22:24:27] sts along the side of Square 1: *see* diagram A. Follow instructions for Square 1 from * to *.

## Square 3

Using col B, pick up 19[22:24:27] sts along side of Square 1. Then cast on 20[23:25:28] sts; *see* diagram A. Follow instructions for Square 1 from * to *.

## Right front

Work Square 1, then Square 2. Follow diagram B to make a column of 6 squares with the decreases facing the way illustrated, then put it on its side and, following the diagram, pick up sts for an inserted 'flare'.

### Flare (right front and left back)

Using col A, with right side facing, pick up and knit 19[22:24:27] sts from the side of each square; so over 6 squares this will be 114[132:144:162] sts. Now shape the 'flare' by using short rows. Knit back 1 row, until 19[22:24:27] sts left before the end of the row, turn and knit back. (See Chapter 6 for how to turn without leaving holes.)
Knit, leaving 19[22:24:27] more sts behind, turn and knit back. Cont in this way, leaving 19[22:24:27] more sts behind on each wrong-side row until you have worked the last 19[22:24:27] sts. Now work longer rows again, beginning on the wrong side: K38[44:48:54], turn, knit back, then K57[66:72:81], turn

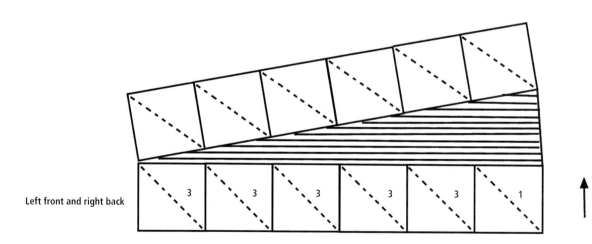

*Pattern 3, diagram B: construction of short-row 'flares'.*

and knit back, and so on, working another 19[22:24:27] sts each time until you have worked all the way across again, finishing on the wrong side.

Leave these sts on a spare circular needle or holder. You can use them for the next column of squares, picking up 19[22:24:27] sts for one side of each square, and 20[23:25:28] from the preceding square: *see* diagram A. Complete the top part of the piece in squares, following the diagram, and where the squares are between others, pick up all the sts from the previous edges. Otherwise, cast on edges where needed, and leave space for the armholes.

## Front neck shaping

(*See* diagram A for position of front neck squares.)
Work a triangle or half-square for front of neck by picking up 20[23:25:28] sts from side of a previous square, working in usual pattern straight across on these sts, decreasing 1 st at neck edge corner on alt rows in place of central decrease.

## Left front and right back

Work Square 1, then Square 3 (so that the decreases face the other way).

*Square 3:* Pick up 19[22:24:27] along side of Square 1: *see* diagram B. Then cast on 20(23:25:28). Follow instructions for Square 1 from * to *.

Now follow the diagram to make a column of 6 as before, but they face in mirror image to the first two pieces.

## Flare (left front and right back)

Using col A, with right side facing, pick up and knit 19[22:24:27] sts from the side of each square; so over 6 squares this will be 114[132:144:162] sts.

Knit back 1 row. This faces the opposite way from flared pieces in the first half. Now shape the 'flare' by using short rows. Knit until 19[22:24:27] sts left before the end of the row, turn and knit back. Knit leaving 19[22:24:27] more sts behind, turn and knit back.

Cont in this way, leaving 19[22:24:27] more sts behind on each right-side row until you have worked the last 19[22:24:27] sts.

Now work longer rows again, beginning K38[44:48:54], turn, knit back, then K57[66:72:81], turn and knit back, and so on, working another 19[22:24:27] sts each time until you have worked all the way across again.

Make a right front and left back.

## Centre back

At the centre of the back, make an extra flare. Either cast off, or leave the sts on a thread so that you can graft them to the other half of back (*see* Chapter 6).

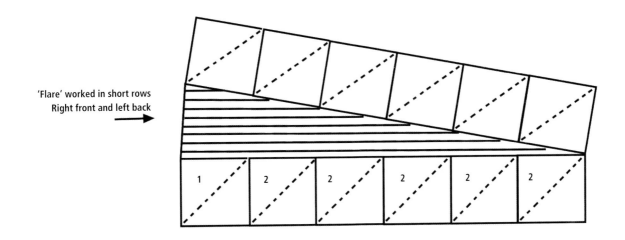

'Flare' worked in short rows
Right front and left back →

## Sleeves

These are worked from the top down. Join the shoulders (*see* Chapter 6 for joining).

With right side of garment facing and col B, pick up the stitches from the bottom of the armhole to the shoulder, then down the other side to armhole, but not across the underarm edge: *see* diagram A. Pick up and knit 20[23:25:28] sts per square (80[92:100:112 over 4 squares).

*Pattern:* * Work in garter st using col B, for 5cm (2in), then change to col C, D or E: see main photo for colour order. Work 4 rows stocking st, then rep from *, in stripes of 5cm (2in) col B, 4 rows col C, D or E. When sleeve measures 20[22:24:26] cm, (8[8½:9½:10]in), decrease 1 st at each end of next and every following 6th row. Continue until sleeve measures 45[47:49:52]cm (17½[18½:19¼:20¾]in) or the length you want, and cast off (in whichever colour you are using).

*Cuff:* If you would like a ribbed cuff, change to size 3mm (US2:UK11) needles and knit one row decreasing to 60 sts, work in K2, P2 rib for 3cm (1¼in) and cast off.

## Neck and bands

*Neck:* Using size 3mm (US2:UK11) needles and col B, pick up and knit 26[29:31:34] sts along slope of right front neck, 22[25:28:31] sts from each square at back of neck, and 26[29:31:34] sts along left front neck. Work in K2, P2 rib for 8 rows, and cast off.

*Front bands:* Using size 3mm (US2:UK11) needles and col B, pick up and knit 22[25:28:31] sts from each square, all along each front edge. Note: the ribbing will pull in slightly, so 22[25:28:31] sts are needed rather than the usual 20[23:25:28]. Work in K2, P2 rib.

*Buttonholes:* Place the buttonholes (*see* Chapter 6) on the right-hand band level with the top of each square, 3 sts wide (adjust size for your chosen buttons). If you prefer, work a plain ribbed band and add crochet loops afterwards. Rib for 8 rows altogether, and cast off.

## Finishing

Join side seams, sleeve seams and underarm seams, and sew on buttons.

## Double squares

This design can be made without side seams and shoulder seams by fitting these double squares in at the sides and over the shoulder. You need to work each piece, front and back, from the centre front towards the sides until you reach the position of the double square that will join the sides, then pick up the stitches from each half front and back to make the joining 'double' square. NB. Follow diagrams B and C for Pattern 1.

Using col B, start with 78[90:98:110] sts, picked up as before from previous squares or cast on where necessary. Knit back one row, then start pattern as before.

**Row 3** K18[21:23:26], S1, K2 tog, psso, K36[42:46:52], S1, K2 tog, psso, K18[21:23:26].

**Row 4** Knit.

**Row 5** K17[20:22:25], S1, K2 tog, psso, K34[40:44:50], S1, K2 tog, psso, K17[20:22:25].

**Row 6** Knit.

**Row 7** Change to col C or D, K16[19:21:24], S1, K2 tog, psso, K32[38:42:48], S1, K2 tog, psso, K16[19:21:24].

**Row 8** Using col C or D, purl.

**Row 9** Using col B, K15[18:20:23], S1, K2 tog, psso, K30[36:40:46] S1, K2 tog, psso, 15[18:20:23].

Cont in this way, in garter st, decreasing on right-side rows, changing col again when you have 18 sts left. Using col E, K3, S1, K2 tog, psso, K6, S1, K2 tog, psso, K3, knit back. Continue decreasing as before, until 6 sts left: S1, K2 tog, psso, S1, K2 tog, psso. K2 tog, break thread and pull thread through.

# Stripy modular jacket

## Materials
4-ply wool, 300g (10½oz) col A (975m), 150g
(5½oz) col B (488m)

## Dyes
Col A: black 1%
Col B: brown 0.25%

## Needles
Size 3.25mm (US3:UK10), 3mm (US2:UK11) for
cuffs, straight or circular (a circular needle is useful
for the top of the sleeve)

## Size
Finished measurement without stretching:
92[96]cm (36[37½]in)

## Tension
Each square needs to measure 7.5[8.5:9.5:10.5]cm
(3[3½:3¾:4¼]in). This allows for a comfortable fit,
not too tight.

## Knitting level
Moderate

*Pattern 4, colour codes.*

## Construction

This jacket is made up from large and small squares, which are linked as they are knitted in the same way as the 'modular squares' jacket, but it is knitted in a springy, stripy welting pattern. See diagram for order of knitting the squares. There are 2 sizes of square. Begin with the larger square.

*Pattern 4, stitch chart.*

Sleeve length 49 [51] cms

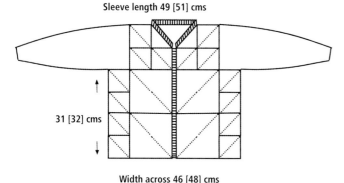

31 [32] cms

Width across 46 [48] cms

*Pattern 4, measurements.*

## Large Square

This begins at centre bottom for back and front.
Using col A, cast on 81[85] sts.

**Row 2\*** Knit.

**Row 3** (Right side) P39[41], P3 tog, P39[41]. Mark the centre with a tag of wool or stitch marker that can travel up the rows with the knitting to remind you where to decrease and keep the decreases in line: this sort of decrease makes a neat diagonal that is part of the design.

**Row 4** Knit.

**Row 5** P38[40], P3 tog, P38[40].

**Row 6** Knit.

**Row 7** Change to col B, K37[39], S1, K2 tog, psso, K37[39].

**Row 8** Purl.

**Row 9** Change to col A, K36[38], S1, K2 tog, psso, K36[38].

**Row 10** Knit.

**Row 11** P35[37], P3 tog, P35[37].

**Row 12** Knit.

**Row 13** Change to col B, K34[36], S1, K2 tog, psso, K34[36].

**Row 14** Purl.

Cont in this way, decreasing on right-side rows, but working 6 rows purl-side stocking st in col A, then 2 rows knit-side stocking st stripe in col B alternately, always knitting the first row when you change col, as at rows 7 and 9.

When there are 3 sts left, S1, K2 tog, psso. Pull thread through and weave in securely or finish off. (*See* Chapter 4 for weaving in ends.)

## Small Square

*Square 2:* Small squares are worked in exactly the same way, beginning with 41[43] sts and using the same stripy ribbed pattern.

Cast on 21[22] sts, then with right side facing, pick up 20[21] along half the side of large square: *see* diagram. Square 2 is half the size of the large square.

Follow instructions for large square from * to *, beginning 'Row 2) Knit, Row 3) P19[20], P3 tog, P19[20]', and always decrease on the centre 3 sts on right-side rows.

*Square 3:* Pick up 20[21] sts along half the side of large square, and cast on 21[22] sts (*see* diagram), and work the same as Square 2.

Now follow the diagram, working large squares where marked, and where the squares are between others, pick up all the sts from the previous edges. Otherwise, cast on edges where needed. Make a separate piece for each front, as in the diagram, shaping only for front neck (*see* diagram).

Work a triangle or half-square for front of neck by picking up 20[21] sts from side of one previous square, working in the usual pattern, and decreasing 1 st at neck edge corner on alt rows in place of the usual central decrease.

## Back

Work in the same way as the front, but the second half of the back can be joined with the first half by picking up stitches, except for the bottom square, which is left open to make a split back.

## Sleeves (worked separately from the top down.)

Join the shoulders (*see* Chapter 6).

With right side of garment facing and col A, pick up the stitches from the bottom of the armhole to the shoulder, then down from other shoulder to armhole, but not across the underarm edge (*see* diagram). Pick up and knit 21[22] sts per square (84[88] sts over the 4 squares).

*Pattern:* The same as for the body: 6 rows purl-side stocking st, 2 rows knit-side stocking st, alternately.

When sleeve measures 30cms (12in), decrease 1 st at each end of next and every following 6th row. Continue until sleeve measures 49[51]cm (19¼[20¼]in). It is difficult to measure as the stitch is so stretchy, but try not to stretch it too much while measuring or the sleeve will be too short. The stretchiness will depend on the yarn used.

*Cuff:* Using 3mm (US2:UK11) needles and col A, work one row, decreasing evenly along the row to 60 sts. Now work in K2, P2 rib for 3cm (1½in), and cast off loosely.

## Neck and bands

*Neck:* Using size 3.25mm (US3:UK10) needles and col A, pick up and knit 24[26] sts along slope of right front neck, 21[23] sts from each square at back of neck, and 24 [26] sts along right front neck. Knit back 1 row.

Work in K2, P2 rib for 6 rows, and cast off.

*Front bands:* Using size 3.25mm (US3:UK10) needles and col A, pick up and knit 24[26] sts from each square, all along each front edge. Knit back1 row. NB the ribbing will pull in slightly, so 24[26] sts are needed rather than the usual 21[23]. Work in K2, P2 rib for 6 rows, and cast off.

*Buttonholes:* Follow instructions in Chapter 6.

## Finishing

Join side seams, sleeve seams and underarm seams, and sew on buttons. *See* Chapter 6, for joining seams.

### Seamless version

Alternatively, you could make this design with double squares so there are no side seams. You need to cast on double the amount of stitches, following the diagrams for the double module in Pattern 1.

For example, after you have made the fronts and back from the centre working towards the position of the double side square: pick up 82[86] sts, and follow the instructions for the small square, repeating each instruction twice along the double row.

Front

Back

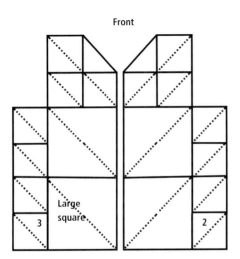
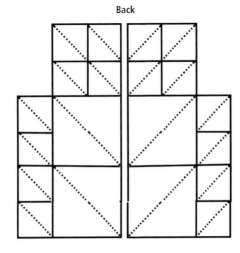
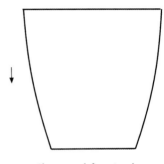

Sleeve: work from top down

*Pattern 4, diagram.*

# Harlequin jacket

## Materials

4-ply wool, 50g (1¾oz) col A (163m), 50g (1¾oz) col B (163m), 150g (5½oz) each of cols C, D, E and F (488m), 50g (1¾oz) col G (163m)

## Dyes

Col A: blue 0.5%, yellow 0.1%
Col B: navy 0.05%, blue 0.15, yellow 0.25%
Col C: black 0.3%, blue 0.3%, yellow 0.1%
Col D: navy 0.4%, blue 1.5%, yellow 1.2%
Col E: blue 2%, yellow 1%
Col F: navy 0.4%, blue 0.4%, yellow 1.2%
Col G: red 1.5%, brown 0.25%

## Needles

Size 3.25mm (US3:UK10), 3 mm (US2:UK11) for cuffs and bands, straight or circular (a circular needle is useful for the top of the sleeve)

## Size

To fit bust 77[81:86]cm (30¼[31¾:34]in) not too tight.

## Knitting level

Moderate. Modular knitting plus inset modules.

## Construction

This is a variation on Pattern 1, but the first row of squares is made as individual squares, unjoined, because others are inset between them at the end. See diagrams for order of knitting the squares, and for the option of knitting without side seams. Make sure to weave the ends in for some distance to secure them before cutting off (*see* Chapter 4 for weaving in ends).

## Square 1

This begins at centre bottom for each back and front piece. Cast on 35[37:39] sts using col A or B (*see* main photo for order of colours). * Knit back 1 row.
**Row 1** Change to col C, D, E or F (*see* main photo for order of colours), K16[17:18], S1, K2 tog, psso, K16[17:18].
**Row 2** Purl.
**Row 3** P15[16:17], dec as before, P15[16:17].
**Row 4** Knit.
**Row 5** K14[15:16], dec as before, K14[15:16].
Cont in this way, working 2 rows purl, 2 rows knit (row 6 will be purl), decreasing every right side row on the centre 3 sts, until there are 9 sts left.
Change to col G, and work every row knit.
Next row) K3, dec next 3 as usual, K3.
Next row) Knit back.
Next row) K1, dec 3, K1, turn. Knit back.
Next row) S1, K2 tog, psso, break off thread and pull thread through. *
Make 12 of these squares separately for the bottom row (*see* diagram B), following main photo as a guide for colours. Now begin the next row of squares, joining to the first ones as in diagram A, checking that the squares face in the same direction as the diagram.

## Square 2

Cast on 17[18:19] sts using col A or B, then with right side facing, pick up 18[19:20] sts along the side of Square 1: *see* diagram A. Follow instructions for Square 1 from * to *.

## Square 3

Using col A or B, pick up 18[19:20] sts along side of Square 1, and cast on 17[18:19] sts (*see* diagram A) and work the same as Square 1.
Now follow the diagram, and where the squares are between others, pick up all the sts from the previous edges. Otherwise, cast on edges where needed.
Make a separate piece for each front, as in the diagram, shaping only for front neck (*see* diagram A for position of front neck squares).

*Pattern 5, colour codes.*

*Pattern 5, stitch chart.*

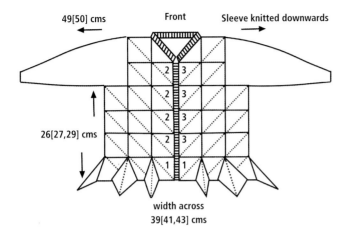

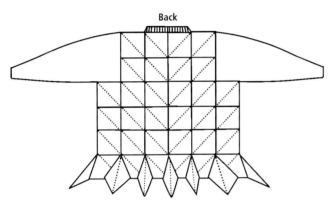

*Pattern 5, diagram A: shape and measurements.*

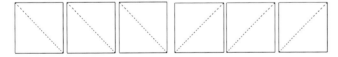

*Pattern 5, diagram B: bottom row of squares.*

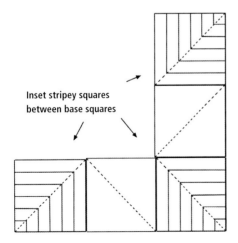

*Pattern 5, diagram C: inset squares.*

Work a triangle or half-square for front of neck by picking up 17[18:19] sts from side of previous square, working in the usual pattern, and decreasing 1 st at neck edge corner on alt rows in place of the usual central decrease.

## Back

Work in the same way as the front, but the second half of the back can be picked up from the first half.

## Insets

*See* diagrams A and C for position of these. They are just like the other squares, but worked in 2-row stripes.

Pick up sts between the existing base squares as before using col A or B, and work in garter stitch 2 rows each of colours A or B alternating with C, D, E or F, decreasing on right-side rows as before. Work inset squares to match the diagram, leaving front edges flat with no insets.

## Sleeves

Sleeves are worked from the top down. Join the shoulders (*see* Chapter 6).

With right side of garment facing and col A, pick up the stitches from the bottom of the armhole to the shoulder, then down from other shoulder to armhole, but not across the underarm edge (see diagram A). Pick up and knit 18[19:20] sts per square (72[76:80] sts over the 4 squares). Knit back 1 row.

*Pattern:* * Knit 2 rows, purl 2 rows, using col C, D, E or F for 12 rows, then work col A, B or G stripe in stocking st for 2 rows, knitting on right side, purling on reverse. * Rep from * to * following main photo for order of colours.

When sleeve measures 30cm (12in), decrease 1 st at each end of next and every following 6th row. Continue until sleeve measures 49[50]cm (19¼[20]in).

*Cuff:* Change to size 3mm (US2:UK11) needles and col D, and work one row, decreasing evenly along the row to 60 sts. Now work in K2, P2 rib in col D for 3cm (1½in), and cast off loosely.

## Front bands

Using size 3mm (US2:UK11) needles and col A, pick up sts along the front edge. You need to pick up several more sts than usual for these borders, as the ribbing pulls in. (If it is easier, increase on the following row, so you end up with 20[21:22] sts per square.)

Knit back 1 row, then join in col D and work in rib.
Next row) K1 col D, P1 col A, keeping yarns on wrong side.
Next row) Keep same cols on same sts and work in rib.

*Buttonholes:* Make buttonholes on the right-hand band level with the top of each square (*see* Chapter 6), or alternatively work a plain ribbed band and add crochet loops afterwards. Rib for 6 rows altogether, and cast off.

## Neck

Using size 3mm (US2:UK11) needles and col A, pick up and knit round the neck, starting at right front. Pick up 24[25:26] sts from the diagonal at right front of neck, then 20[21:22] sts from each square at back of neck, and another 24[25:26] sts from the diagonal at left front of neck (88[92:96] sts).
Knit back 1 row, then using colours D and A, work in rib.
Next row) * K1 col D, P1 col A *, and rep, keeping yarns on wrong side.
Next row) Keep same cols on same sts and work in rib for 6 rows, then cast off using col A.

## Finishing

Join side seams, sleeve seams and underarm seams, and sew on buttons. *See* 'Finishing', Chapter 6 for sewn seams.

### Seamless version

Alternatively, you could make this design with double squares so there are no side seams. You need to cast on double the amount of stitches, following diagram C for Pattern 1.
For example, working the first squares as written from the centre towards the sides, when you reach the position of the side 'double' squares, double the instructions:
Using col A or B (see main photo for order of colours), pick up 70[74:78] sts. * Knit back 1 row using A or B. The bottom double square will be cast on, not picked up.
**Row 1** Change to col C, D, E or F (*see* main photo for order of colours). * K16[17:18], S1, K2 tog, psso, K16[17:18] *; rep from * to *.
**Row 2** Purl.
Cont from row 3, repeating the instructions along the double row.

*Detail of squares inset by picking up stitches and knitting downwards at the end.*

# Classic squares jacket

## Materials

4-ply wool 50g (1¾oz) col A (163m), 500–600g
(18–21oz) col B (1,625–1,950m), 50g (1¾oz) col C
(163m), 150g (5½oz) col D (488m)

## Dyes

Col A: black 0.2%, blue 0.2%, yellow 0.1%
Col B: black 0.05%, blue 0.1%
Col C: blue 0.05%
Col D: brown 0.5%

## Needles

Size 3.25mm (US3:UK10), and size 3mm
(US2:UK11) for bands, straight or circular (a circular

needle is useful for the top of the sleeve).

## Size

Actual garment measurement: 101[107:112]cm
(39½[42:44]in)

## Tension

Small square should measure 6.3[6.7:7]cm
(2½[2⅝:2¾]in)

## Knitting level

Moderate/advanced: modular knitting with larger
areas of mitred knitting.

## Construction

This jacket is made up from different sized mitred squares that are linked as they are knitted. *See* diagram A for placing of the different squares. The instructions are given for knitting separate backs and fronts, but following directions at the end of the pattern, you could use the same method to knit each half front joined with a half back and no side seams.

The jacket starts with some right-angled stripes, followed by 2 sizes of square; *see* diagram A.

## Angled stripes

The cast-on edge makes all of the bottom edge and part of the front edge of the jacket.

Using col A, cast on 135[141:147] sts and knit back one row.

**Row 3** (Right side) Using col B, K66[69:72], K3 tog, K66[69:72]. Mark the centre with a tag of wool or stitch marker that can travel up the rows with the knitting to remind you where to decrease and keep the decreases in line: it makes a neat diagonal that is part of the design.

**Row 4** Knit.

**Row 5** P65[68:71], P3 tog, P65[68:71].

**Row 6** Knit.

**Row 7** Change to col D, K64[67:70], S1, K2 tog, p2sso, K64[67:70].

**Row 8** Purl.

**Row 9** Change to col B, K63[66:69], S1, K2 tog, p2sso, K63[66:69].

**Row 10** Knit.

**Row 11** P62[65:68], P3 tog, P62[65:68].

**Row 12** Knit.

**Row 13** P61[64:67], P3 tog, P61[64:67].

**Row 14** Knit.

Continue in this way, decreasing on the centre 3 sts on right-side rows, following pattern rows 7–14. NB the colour change is always a knit row on the right side.

Carry on until you have decreased to 95[101:107] sts.

## Large Square 1

Now continue in garter st with decreases as before, using col B, until 9 sts left. Change to col C and continue until all the sts have gone. Fasten off end.

There is 1 large square on each front and half back.

## Small Square

Small squares are joined to the large square and worked in exactly the same way, with the first two rows knitted to make an edge in col A, beginning with 33[35,37] sts. Change to

*Pattern 6, colour codes.*

 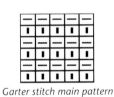

Angled stripes.  Garter stitch main pattern

*Pattern 6, stitch charts.*

col B and knit in garter st throughout using col B until there are 9 sts left, then work the rest of the square in col C.

## Square 2

Using col A, cast on 17[18:19] sts, then with right side facing, pick up 16[17:18] sts evenly along the side of the neighbouring square or the stripes: see diagram A.
One side of the small square fits 3 times into the large square, and fits across the angled stripes, picking up 1 st to each 'ridge' or 2 rows of knitting.
Knit back 1 row, * then change to col B and K15[16:17], K3 tog, K15[16:17].
Work in garter st using col B. On every right-side row, work to 1 st before centre, and K3 tog. Carry on until 9 sts left. Change to col C and continue until all the sts have gone. *

## Square 3

Using col A, with right side facing, pick up 16[17:18] sts evenly along the side of the neighbouring square or the stripes, and cast on 17[18:19] sts, and knit back 1 row (*see* diagram A). Work the same as Square 2 from * to *.

## Square 4

Using col A, pick up 16[17:18] sts along side of Square 2 or previous square, 1 at the corner, and 16[17:18] sts along side of Square 1, and knit back 1 row (*see* diagram A). Work the same as Square 2 from * to *.
Now follow the diagram, and where the squares are between others, pick up all the sts from the previous edges. Otherwise, cast on edges where needed.
Make a separate piece for each front, as in the diagram.

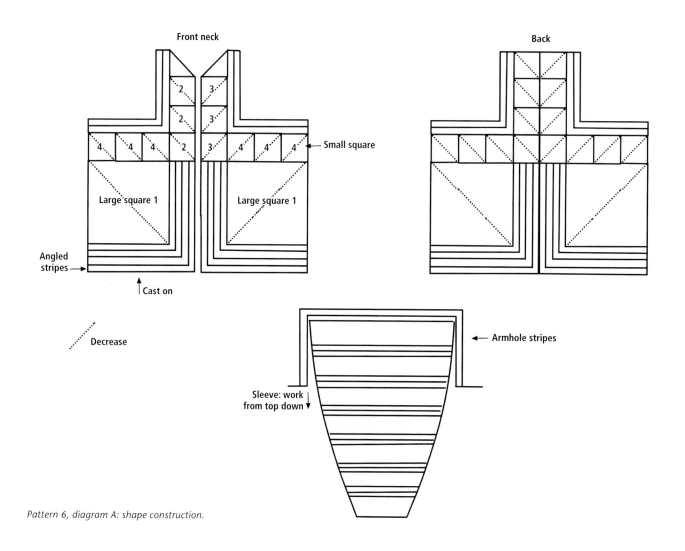

*Pattern 6, diagram A: shape construction.*

## Front neck shaping

See diagram A for position of front neck squares. Work a triangle or half-square for front of neck by picking up 16[17:18] sts from side of one previous square, working in the usual pattern, and decreasing 1 st at neck edge corner on alt rows in place of the usual central decrease.

## Back

Work in the same way as the front, with no neck shaping. The second half of the back can be joined by picking up from the first half, leaving the bottom few centimetres (inches) unjoined (casting on instead of picking up) if you want a split at the back.

## Armhole stripes

The stitches for these are going to be picked up from the front and the back on each side, which will join them together at the shoulder: *see* diagram A.

Beginning under the arm and using col A, pick up 16[17:18] sts from each of the 3 squares under the arm, 1 st from the corner, and 16[17:18] sts from each of the 3 squares up the left front edge of the armhole, then the same again from the corresponding left back, 1 st from the corner, and 16[17:18] sts from the 3 squares under the arm (194[206:218] sts). Knit back one row.

**Row 3** (Right side) Using col B, * K47[50:53], K3 tog (corner), K47[50:53] *; rep from * to *. Mark the decrease with a tag of wool or stitch marker that can travel up the rows with the knitting to remind you where to decrease and keep the decreases in line.

**Row 4** Knit.
**Row 5** * P46[49:52], P3 tog, P46[49:52] *; rep from * to *.
**Row 6** Knit.
**Row 7** Change to col D, * K45[48:51], S1, K2tog, p2sso, K45[48:51] *; rep from * to *.
**Row 8** Purl.
**Row 9** Change to col B, * K44[47:50], S1, K2tog, p2sso, K44[47:50] *; rep from * to *.
**Row 10** Knit.
**Row 11** * P43[46:49], P3 tog, P43[46:49] *; rep from * to *.
**Row 12** Knit.
**Row 13** * P42[45:48], P3 tog, P42[45:48] *; rep from * to *.
**Row 14** Knit.

Put the sts under the arm on a spare thread or stitch holder, and keep the armhole sts on a holder to use for the sleeve. Work the other armhole the same, for the right front and right back.

## Sleeves

With right side of garment facing and col B, pick up the stitches from the bottom of the armhole to the shoulder, then down from shoulder to armhole, but not across the underarm edge: *see* diagram A.

*Pattern:* * Work 5cm (2in) in garter st using col B, then 2 bands of: 6 rows purl-side stocking st, 2 rows knit-side stocking st using col C or D, alternately. * Rep from * to * all down sleeve.

When sleeve measures 35cm (13¾in), decrease 1 st at each end of next and every following 6th row. Continue until sleeve measures 48[50:52]cm (18¾[20:20¾]in) or the length you want, and cast off.

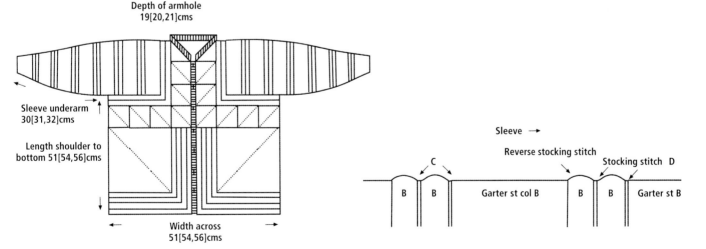

*Pattern 6, diagram B: measurements.*

*Pattern 6, diagram C: sleeve pattern.*

## Neck and bands

*Neck:* Using size 3mm (US2:UK11) needles and col A, starting at right front of neck, pick up and knit 19[21:23] sts along slope of front neck, 17[18:19] sts from each square at back of neck, and 19[21:23] more sts along left front neck. Knit back 1 row.

Change to col B and work in K2, P2 rib for 8 rows, and cast off in rib using col A.

*Front bands:* Using size 3mm (US2:UK11) needles col A, pick up and knit 21 sts from each square, all along each front edge. The ribbing will pull in slightly, so 19[21:23] sts are needed rather than the usual 17[18:19]. Knit back 1 row. Work in K2, P2 rib.

*Buttonholes:* Make buttonholes (*see* Chapter 6) on the right-hand band according to the size of your chosen buttons, level with the top of each small square, and equally spaced down the front, with the bottom one a small square's length from the bottom.

Rib for 8 rows altogether, making the buttonholes on row 5, and cast off using col A.

## Finishing

Start with the underarm join, put the sts from the holder onto a spare double-ended knitting needle, and join as described in Chapter 6. Join side seams and sleeve seams, and sew on buttons.

## Suggestions

This design can be made without side seams by fitting these double squares in at the sides, following diagram D.

You need to cast on double the amount of stitches, and repeat the instructions for each row.

For example, beginning with the angles stripes, cast on 270[282:294] sts using col A, and knit back one row.

**Row 3** (Right side) Using col B, * K66[69:72], K3 tog, K66[69:72] *; rep from * to *. Mark the decreases with a tag of wool or stitch marker that can travel up the rows with the knitting to help keep the decreases in line: they make a neat diagonal that is part of the design.

**Row 4** Knit.

**Row 5** * P65[68:71], P3 tog, P65[68:71] *; rep from * to *.

**Row 6** Knit.

**Row 7** Change to col D, * K64[67:70], S1, K2 tog, p2sso, K64[67:70]*; rep from * to *.

Continue following the main pattern given above (from row 8), repeating the instructions for each row to make the double-angled stripes, and then the double squares.

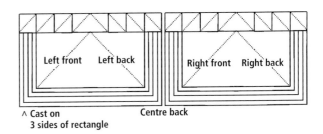

∧ Cast on
3 sides of rectangle

Centre back

*Pattern 6, diagram D: seamless version.*

*Pattern 6, some different colourways.*

# Shell jacket

## Materials

4-ply wool, main colours F to K, dot colours A to E
25g (1oz) each cols A to E (82m), 100g (3½oz) each cols F
to J (325m), 150g (5½oz) col K (488m)

## Dyes

Col A: red 0.1%, blue 0.04%
Col B: red 0.75%, navy 0.05%
Col C: red 0.3%, brown 0.075%
Col D: yellow 0.5%, navy 0.01%, brown 0.01%
Col E: navy 0.4%, blue 0.4%, yellow 1.2%
Col F: blue 0.1%, yellow 0.15%, black 0.05%
Col G: yellow 0.25%, navy 0.01%, brown 0.01%
Col H: blue 0.1%, yellow 0.1%, brown 0.01%
Col I: navy 0.05%, blue 0.3%, yellow 0.25%
Col J: navy 0.05%, blue 0.15%, yellow 0.25%
Col K: blue 0.2%, yellow 0.3%, black 0.1%

## Needles

Size 3.25mm (US3:UK10) straight or circular, and 3mm
(US2:UK11) for front bands

## Size

Each module is 11.5[12.5]cm (4½[5]in) wide, and 8[8.5]
cm (3[3¼]in) high.
This is a loose-fitting jacket, that will fit bust size130[142]
cm (51[55¾]in). *See* diagram for measurements.

## Knitting level

Moderate/advanced

*Pattern 7, colour codes.*

## Construction

This jacket is made up from scallop-shapes that are linked as they are knitted. The shapes are cast on, or picked up from previous scallops, and decrease every few rows in four places, making the curved shape. The modules join the sleeve to the body so there are no sewn seams. *See* diagram for order of knitting the modules.

## Basic module

Using col K, cast on 31[34] sts. Knit 3 rows (garter st).

§ With right side facing, make the decreases in the next row like this:

Next row) K2 tog, * K7[8], S1, K2tog, psso *; rep from * to *, K7[8], S1, K1, psso.

Next row) Purl.

Work 4 rows in stocking st.

Next dec row) K2 tog, * K5[6], S1, K2tog, psso *; rep from * to *, K5[6], S1, K1, psso.

Next row) (Wrong side) Knit (this makes a 'ridge').

Work 4 rows in stocking st.

Next dec row) K2 tog, * K3[4], S1, K2tog, psso *; rep from * to *, K3[4], S1, K1, psso.

Next row) Knit.

Work 4 rows in stocking st.

Next dec row) K2 tog, * K1[2], S1, K2 tog, psso *; rep from * to *, K1[2], S1, K1, psso (7[10] sts).

Next row) Knit.

Work 4 rows stocking st.

Change to 'dot' colour (any col from A to E): see main photo for order of colours.

Next dec row) K2 tog, S1, K2 tog, psso, [S1, K2 tog, psso again for larger size], S1, K1, psso.

Purl these 3[4] sts, then S1, K1, psso [K2 tog, S1, K1, psso for larger size].

Next row) Purl these 2 sts.

K2 tog and break off yarn and pull through.

Make 12 modules for the bottom of the jacket, and then the next row of modules can all be picked up from these.

## Picking up

Begin at the cast-off tip, pick up and knit 15[17] sts along the edge to the bottom (*see* diagram and follow main photo for order of colours) and 16[17] sts beginning at the bottom of the next module, finishing at the cast-off tip (31[34] sts). Knit back 1 row, then knit 2 more rows. Work as for the first module from §.

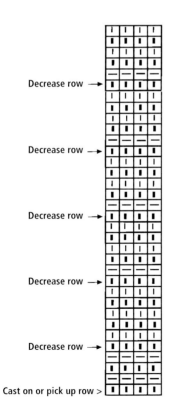

Decrease row →
Decrease row →
Decrease row →
Decrease row →
Decrease row →
Cast on or pick up row >

*Pattern 7, stitch chart.*

**NB** Weave the ends in when picking up the sts for the next module, or sew in afterwards. There is a danger that it can unravel if cut off too short.

## Half-modules

You will see from the diagram that there have to be half-modules to make the front edge of the jacket. These are picked up as before. For right front of jacket they are picked up from bottom of previous module to tip (15[17]) sts.
Work the usual garter st edge, then work the decs as follows:
Next row) K3[4], S1, K2 tog, psso, K7[8], S1, K1, psso.
Next row) Purl, then work 4 more rows in stocking st.
Next dec row) K2[3], S1, K2 tog, psso, K5[6], S1, K1, psso.
Next row) Knit.
Work 4 rows in stocking st.
Next dec row) K1[2], S1, K2 tog, psso, K3[4], S1, K1, psso.
Next row) Knit.
Work 4 rows in stocking st.
Next dec row) K0[1], S1, K2 tog, psso, K1[2], S1, K1, psso.
Next row) Knit.
Work 4 rows in stocking st, then change to 'dot' colour.
Next dec row) For smaller size, finish off. For larger size, S1, K2 tog, psso, S1, K1, psso.
Try and continue to make the tip as long as the whole shapes, and finish off.

## Left front half-modules

Pick up 15[17] sts from tip to base of previous module. Work the garter st edge, and then K2 tog, K7[8], S1, K2 tog, psso, K3[4].
Next row) Purl.

Work 4 rows in stocking st.
Next dec row) K2 tog, K5[6], S1, K2 tog, psso, K2[3].
Next row) Knit (this makes a 'ridge').
Work 4 rows in stocking st.
Next dec row) K2 tog, K3[4], S1, K2 tog, psso, K1[2].
Next row) Knit.
Work 4 rows in stocking st.
Next dec row) K2 tog, K1[2], S1, K2tog, psso, K0[1].
Next row) Knit.
Work 4 rows in stocking st, then change to 'dot' colour.
Next dec row) For smaller size, K2 tog, S1, K1. For larger size, K2 tog, S1, K2 tog, psso.
Try and continue to make the tip as long as the whole modules, and finish off.
Now follow the diagram to make the body, with the shell-shapes travelling up at a 'raglan sleeve'-type angle, and also leaving a gap for the neck, with a half-module at either side of front neck.

## Centre back neck

Work module in the same way but decrease at the edges every right-side row, and cast off on row 6 instead of continuing to a point. This will flatten the top of the shape at the centre back of neck.

## Sleeves

These are picked up from the top of the shoulder and worked downwards, starting from the neck. Pick up the stitches from the edges of the body shell-shapes as before. The first module will join the back with the half-module at front of neck. The sleeves can be worked in the round once the top of the sleeve is joined in.

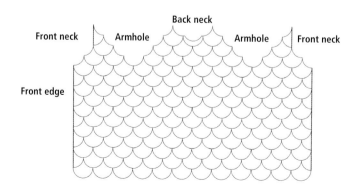

*Pattern 7, diagram and measurements.*

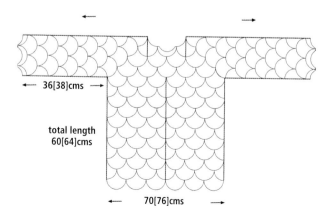

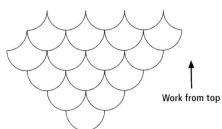

*Pattern 7, sleeve top.*

*Detail of bottom edge.*

When sleeve measures about 40–43cm (14½[16¾]in) under the arm, cast off the last round of modules on row 6 (instead of going to a point) as in the diagram.

## Neck and bands

*Front bands*: Using size 3mm (US2:UK11) needles and col K, pick up and knit sts from each half-module, all along each front edge. NB the ribbing will pull in slightly, so make sure you pick up 16–18 sts from each half module. Work in K2, P2 rib for 8 rows, and cast off.

*Buttonholes: See* Chapter 6: make these on row 3 of the band.

*Neck:* Beginning on the right side at right neck edge, using size 3mm (US2:UK11) needles and col K, pick up and knit 20 sts per module. Work in K4, P4 rib, decreasing every 4th row. 1st dec: on each group of K4, (K1, K2 tog, K1, then P4); rep to end.
Cont to work ribbing for 3 rows:
**Row 1** (P3, K4); rep.
**Row 2** (K3, P4); rep.
**Row 3** (P3, K4); rep.
Next decrease: Decrease on the purl sts to make K3, P3. Work 4 rows, decrease to K2, P3, work 4 rows, decrease to K2, P2. After 16 rows, cast off using col K.

## Finishing

Join the underarm modules, sew in ends and attach buttons.
*Cuffs:* Sew the edges of the short modules together; this gathers in the sleeve at the wrist.

# Entrelac jumper, ribbed

## Materials

4-ply wool, 475[525:550:600:650]g (17[19:20:21:23]oz) col B (1,545m [1,706m, 1,788m, 1,950m, 2,112m]), and 50g (1¾oz) of col A (163m) to cast on and use for edging the neck and cuffs. Col A = contrast, col B = main colour

## Dyes

Col A: black 0.5%, dip-dyed
Col B: brown 0.1%, black 0.05%, unevenly dyed

## Needles

Circular size 3.25mm (US3:UK10), 1 x 80cm (32in), 1 x 40cm (16in), and 1 set of 4 double-ended needles size 3.25mm (US3:UK10). Stitch holders or safety pins.

## Size

Finished chest measurement without stretching (but it is very stretchy): 84[92:100:108:116]cm (32¾[36:39¼:42½:45½]in)

Length: 46[52:56:60:65]cm (18[20¾:22½:23½:25½]in) from shoulder to bottom of zigzag edge. In this design, the smaller sizes automatically end up shorter in proportion. To alter the length: More blocks could be added before the armholes, but you would need to add 2 more rows of blocks in order to follow the instructions from above the armholes. (If one row is added, reverse all the instructions for right and wrong side.)

## Tension

It is difficult to measure the tension of the width in ribbing as it is so stretchy, but check the length by working a strip of ribbing on 16 stitches; the tension should be 48 rows to 12.5cm (5in). Adjust the needle size if necessary or follow the section on sizing in the introduction to this chapter.

## Knitting level

Advanced – practise entrelac first (*see* Chapter 2).

*Pattern 8, colour codes.*

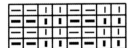

*Pattern 8, stitch chart.*

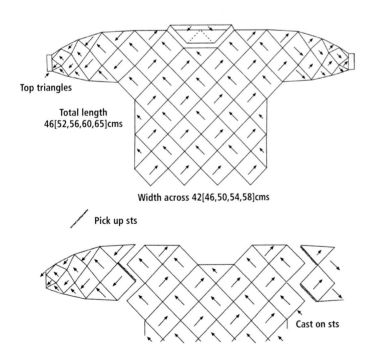

**Top triangles**

**Total length**
**46[52,56,60,65]cms**

**Width across 42[46,50,54,58]cms**

╱ **Pick up sts**

**Cast on sts**

*Pattern 8, diagram A: measurements.*

## Construction

Entrelac, sometimes called 'basket weave' stitch, gives the illusion of a woven fabric. Each module has twice as many rows as there are stitches, and the ribbing makes each 'block' look long and narrow. The bottom edge starts off with whole modules, and as they lie diagonally, this gives a zigzag edge.

## First row of ribbed blocks

Using longer circular needle and col A, cast on 20[22:24:26:28] sts and * purl 1 row.

Change to col B. Work in K2, P2 rib on these 20[22:24:26:28] sts, for 39[43:47:51:55] rows. First block is now complete.

Leaving these sts on the needle, put needle in left hand, join in col A, and cast on 20[22:24:26:28] sts. Rep from * to make 8 blocks altogether.

Don't worry about the appearance of these blocks on the needle; the corner of each one will be hitched up, but it will sort itself out in the following row of blocks.

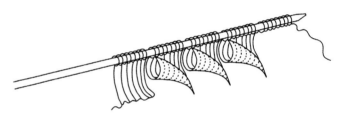

*Pattern 8, diagram B: first row of blocks on needle.*

Break off col B and secure end. Slip last set of sts onto other end of needle.

## Second round of blocks

With right side facing, using col B, * pick up and knit 20[22:24:26:28] sts down side of last block between the points of the needles. Turn.

**Row 1** Working in K2, P2 rib, S1, rib 19[21:23:25:27], turn.
**Row 2** S1, rib 18[20:22:24:26], K2 tog through back of loops (this is the last st + 1st st of the block from the row below).

Rep these 2 rows 19[21:23:25:27] times more until you have joined in all the sts from the block below. Don't turn and work back, but start again from *, and continue all round from * until all blocks are complete in this round. Break off wool and secure.

Note: make sure there are no twists in the work before working the last block.

## Third round of blocks

* With wrong side facing and using col B, pick up and purl 20[22:24:26:28] sts down the side of the block between the needle points. Turn.

**Row 1** Working in K2, P2 rib, S1, rib 19[21:23:25:27], turn.

**Row 2** S1, rib 18[20:22:24:26], P2 tog (this is the last st + 1st st of block in row below), turn.

Rep these 2 rows 19[21:23:25:27] times more. *

Rep from * to * until you have completed the round of 8 blocks.

## Fourth round of blocks

Work as for second round.

## Fifth round of blocks

Work as for third round.

## Divide for armholes

### Back

*First row of blocks:* * Put half the blocks (4) on a stitch holder and work on the other 4 for the back.

With wrong side facing and using col B, cast on 20[22:24:26:28] sts loosely.

**Row 1** Rib.

**Row 2** S1, rib 18[20:22:24:26] sts, K2 tog through back of loops (tbl).

Cont as on round 2 of body until 4 blocks are complete, then make a fifth that fits underarm.

*Block 5:* Pick up and knit 20[22:24:26:28] sts, work 40[44:48:52:56] rows in rib. Break off wool and secure, and put this set of sts on a stitch holder.

*Second row of blocks:* With wrong side facing and col B, pick up and purl 20[22:24:26:28] sts along side of block just worked.

Cont as on round 3 of body until 4 blocks are complete. Break off wool and secure end.

*Third row of blocks:* Work as for first row of blocks from * but cast off sts on last rows of blocks 1 and 4, or leave stitches on a holder to join later.

*Fourth row of blocks:* Triangles for neck shaping are worked on the centre 2 blocks. Leave out the first and last block (putting any spare stitches on holders for grafting).

*First triangle:* With wrong side facing and using col B, pick up and purl 21[23:25:27:29] sts along side of the first 'neck' block (see diagrams A and C).

**Row 1** S1, rib to last 2 sts, K2 tog tbl.

**Row 2** K1, rib 18[20:22:24:26] sts, P2 tog.

Cont decreasing in this way until 1 st remains, making sure you keep rib as set in row 1.

*Second triangle:* With wrong side facing, pick up and purl 20[22:24:26:28] sts, making 21[23:25:27:29] sts on the needle. Work as first triangle until 1 st remains. Break off wool and secure.

### Front

Slide sts back onto needle and work rows of blocks as for rows 1 and 2 for back.

*Third row of blocks:* Work 2 blocks as on row 1, leaving sts on a stitch holder for neck.

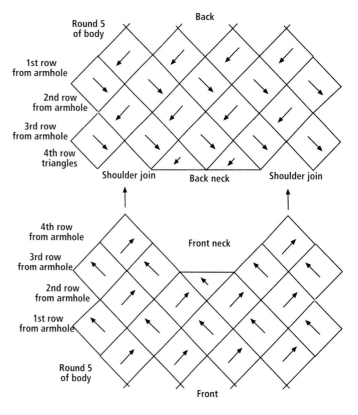

*Pattern 8, diagram C: shoulder join.*

| | First round | Second round | Third round | Fourth round | Fifth round | Sixth round | Seventh round |
|---|---|---|---|---|---|---|---|
| First size | 20 sts | 20 sts | 20 sts | 18 sts | 18 sts | 16 sts | 14 sts |
| Second size | 22 sts | 20 sts | 20 sts | 18 sts | 18 sts | 16 sts | 14 sts |
| Third size | 24 sts | 22 sts | 20 sts | 18 sts | 18 sts | 16 sts | 14 sts |
| Fourth size | 26 sts | 23 sts | 20 sts | 18 sts | 16 sts | 16 sts | 14 sts |
| Fifth size | 28 sts | 25 sts | 22 sts | 19 sts | 16 sts | 14 sts | 14 sts |

*Sleeve chart.*

*Front neck triangle:* Pick up and knit 21[23:25:27:29] sts.
**Row 1** S1, rib to last 2 sts, K2 tog.
**Row 2** K1, rib 18[20:22:24:26] sts, K2 tog tbl.
Cont decreasing until 1 st remains. Count this as first st of next block. Complete 2 more blocks as for first row of blocks from *.

*Fourth row of blocks:* With wrong side facing, using col B, work 1 block only each side for shoulders, as shown on diagram C, keeping stitches on holders to graft to the back. *See* diagram for how it fits together, and graft stitches as described in Chapter 6.

## Neck rib
Put sts from second block of third row of front onto the needle again.
With right side facing and using col A, knit the sts on the holder, pick up and knit 28[29:33:36:38] sts evenly across front triangle, 20[22:24:26:28] sts from side of next block, and 28[29:33:36:38] sts evenly across each of the 2 back neck triangles (124[132:148:160:172] sts). Purl 1 round using col A, then change to col B and work 2.5cm (1in) in K2, P2 rib. Cast off loosely in rib using col A.

## Sleeves
The sleeves are worked in rounds of 3 blocks, picked up from the body at the top and worked downwards.
Slide 2 sets of sts from st holders at the armhole onto short circular needle and pick up 20[22:24:26:28] loops from cast-on sts from the remaining block to make the third set of sts.

The blocks need to decrease in size to shape the sleeve. This is done by decreasing evenly on the last row of every block to the number of sts needed for the next round, and picking up a smaller number of sts along the side of the blocks. First and alternate rows are begun with right side facing, using col B. Second and alternate rows are begun with wrong side facing. The sizes of the blocks are different for each size, so are given separately. Follow your size across for the number of stitches per block in each round.

The seventh round is 3 triangles. Begin by picking up and purling 14 sts, and work as for triangles at back of neck.

*Cuffs:* First, in order to get the number of stitches needed for the cuff, fold the neck ribbing round your wrist and count the stitches for the size of cuff you want. The number needs to be divisible by 4 for the ribbing.
Using col A, and set of 4 double-ended needles, pick up and knit the number of stitches you require evenly from the 3 triangles. Purl 1 row, then change to col B and work 6cm (2¼in) in K2, P2 rib. Cast off loosely in rib using col A.

*Alternative cuff:* To finish with a pointed edge to match the bottom, omit the triangles and cuff, leaving the blocks to shape the edge.

*Pattern 8, a variation in entrelac using the same structure with smaller blocks in stocking stitch.*

This shows another version of entrelac, made with smaller, stocking stitch blocks in a variety of colours.

The blocks are 10 sts wide, with 16 blocks used to make the width of the jumper. Entrelac stocking stitch still makes a very stretchy jumper, with a more raised texture than the ribbed entrelac.

The colours are used in a random order, and the V-neck fits into the construction of the pattern.

The sleeves are 'grown on' in the same way as the ribbed version, and use 8 blocks round the width.

*RIGHT: Pattern 8: neck shaping fits into the entrelac structure.*

# Wrap jacket – short version

## Materials

4-ply wool, 300g–400g (10½–14oz) col A (975–1,300m), 100g (3½oz) col B (325m), 100g (3½oz) col C (325m)

## Dyes

Col A: red 0.2%, blue 0.4%, brown 0.1%
Col B: navy 0.5%, red 0.75%
Col C: navy 1%, red 0.3%, tie-dyed with white fleck

## Needles

Size 3.25mm (US3:UK10)

## Size

This jacket is 3 diagonal squares wide. The finished measurement is 110[124:138]cm (43[48½;54]in) around the width, making a loose, drapey jacket as the knitted fabric is on the bias, and the ribby pattern makes it stretchy.

## Tension

26 sts to 10cm (4in)

## Knitting level

Advanced. This is 'entrelac' knitting (*see* Chapter 2) on a grand scale with each block composed of 'welting' stripes.

## Construction

The jacket is knitted in entrelac technique, a row of squares at a time, joined by picking up. The sleeves are knitted separately and sewn in at the end.

## Back

Using col A, cast on 40[45:50] sts.

Right side facing:

**Rows 1 and 2** Knit.

**Row 3** Purl.

**Row 4** Knit.

Change to col B or C (B and C are mixed randomly, see main picture for colour order).

**Row 5** Knit.

**Row 6** Purl.

Rep these 6 rows throughout all the squares.

Work in this pattern for 80(90:100) rows.

Leaving these sts on the needle, put needle in left hand and cast on 40[45:50] more sts using col A, and work in pattern from row 1. Go on making these squares until you have 5 made.

Don't worry about the appearance of these blocks on the needle; the corner of each one will be hitched up, but it will sort itself out in the following row of blocks.

Break off col B and secure end. Slip last set of sts onto other end of needle.

## Second row of squares

Cast on 40[45:50] more sts using col A, * work in pattern as before, but work the last 2 sts of every right-side row tog (in knit or purl as appropriate).

Work until all the sts of the previous square are joined in (should be 80[90:100] rows).

Continuing with col A, pick up and knit 40[45:50] sts down the side of the next square, and rep from *.

There will be 6 of these squares, the last being picked up from the edge of the first square. *See* diagram A for how all this fits together.

## Third row of squares

Turn work to wrong side and work this row from this side.

Cast on 40[45:50] sts for first square, and you are now joining on the wrong side rows, to join in with the last square of row 2.

Make the square as usual following the pattern below from * row 2, but to make the pattern as before, reverse the knits and purls because you begin on the wrong side.

*Pattern 9, colour codes.*

*Pattern 9, stitch chart.*

*Pattern 9, diagram A: first row of squares on needle.*

For the rest of row 3 squares, pick up and purl 40[45:50] sts down side of previous square using col A (this is the cast-on row of the first square).

**\* Row 2** Purl.

**Row 3** S1, K38[43:48], P2 tog (last st + first st of next square), turn.

**Row 4** Purl. Change to col B or C.

**Row 5** Purl (purling the last 2 together to join as before).

**Row 6** Knit.

Rep until 7 squares are made in this row of squares, keeping the stitches at armholes on a stitch holder.

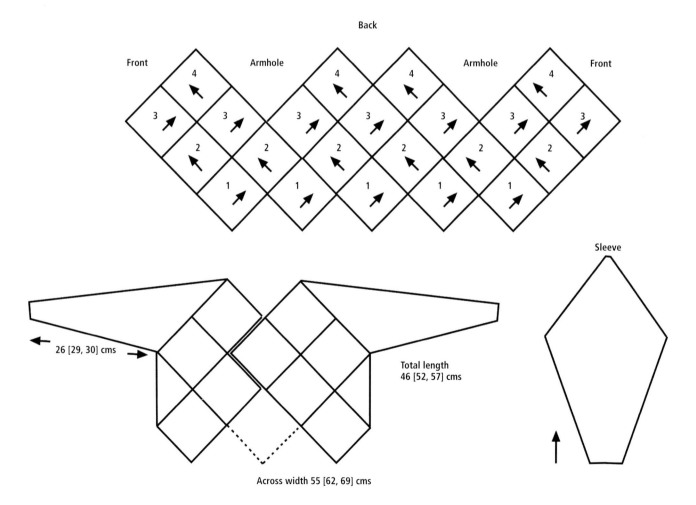

*Pattern 9, diagram B: measurements.*

## Fourth row of squares

Turn and make 4 more, placed as in the diagram by picking up the stitches each time, following the stitch pattern from the second row of squares, and leaving gaps for armholes, keeping the groups of stitches on holders to use for the neckband.

## Sleeves

These are worked separately in K2, P2 rib, in stripes.
Cast on 80 sts using col A, and work in K2, P2 rib in stripes of 4 rows col A, 2 rows col B or C, increasing 1 st at each end of every 6th row until it measures 26[29:30]cm (10[11¼:12]in). Now begin to decrease, at each end of every 4th row for 4 decs, then alternate rows (on right-side rows), in this way: K1, S1, K1, psso, rib to last 3 sts, K2 tog, K1.
Continue until sleeve measures the same as the edge of the 2 squares at the armhole, and put the stitches on a holder for the neck. (You will find that almost all the sts are decreased and there may be none left at this length.) Sew in all ends.

## Neck

Using col A, pick up 40[45:50] sts per square, starting at base of front flap. On the edge of the ribbed squares, pick up 2 sts per 'ridge' and 1 st per 'furrow' to give the right number.
Knit back 1 row, then rib the back of neck section (K2 col C, P2 col A), but work in plain stocking st (col A) for the front sections, decreasing every right-side row on each of the 'corners' (at top of sleeves and centre back): S1, K2 tog, psso. Work for 3cm (1¼in) and cast off.

## Finishing

Fold the plain front bands under and hem in place, grading the band up at the sides where it meets the ribbed back of the neck, which stands up.
Sew the sleeves in place, joining to the stitches on holders (*see* Chapter 6), with the sleeve decrease edge fitting to two 'squares' of the body.
Attach buttons and crochet loops after trying the jacket on and deciding where the buttons need to be placed.

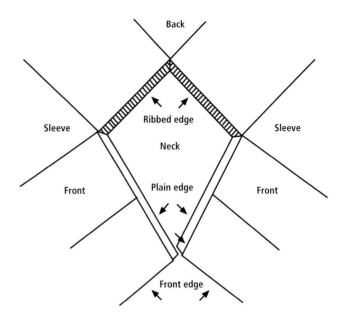

*Pattern 9, diagram C: neck.*

*Detail of neck and fastening.*

# Wrap jacket – long version

## Materials

As for the short version, with 4-ply wool, 500g–600g (18–21oz) col A (975–1,300m), 100g (3½oz) col B (325m),100g (3½oz) col C (325m)

## Dyes

Col A: black 0.5%, yellow 1%

Col B: red 0.5%, yellow 2.5%, brown 0.5%

Col C: red 1%, yellow 3%, brown 0.5%

## First row of squares

Using col A, cast on 40[45:50] sts.

Right side facing:

**Rows 1 and 2** Knit.

**Row 3** Purl.

**Row 4** Knit.

Change to col B or C (B are C are mixed randomly all over: see main photo for order of colours).

**Row 5** Knit.

**Row 6** Purl.

Rep these 6 rows throughout all the squares.

Work in this pattern for 80(90:100) rows.

Leaving these sts on the needle, break off cols and put needle in left hand. Cast on 40[45:50] more sts using col A, and work in pattern from row 1. Go on making these squares until you have 4 made.

Don't worry about the appearance of these blocks on the needle; the corner of each one will be hitched up, but it will sort itself out in the following row of blocks.

Break off col B and secure end. Slip last set of sts onto other end of needle.

*Pattern 9, colour codes.*

*Pattern 9, stitch chart.*

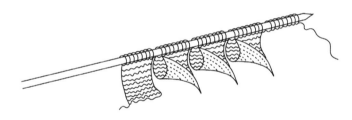

*Pattern 9, first row of squares on needle.*

## Second row of squares

Using col A, cast on 40[45:50] more sts, * work in pattern as before, but work the last st of every right-side row tog (in knit or purl as appropriate) with the 1st st of the neighbouring square from the first row of squares, to join them together.

Work until all the sts of the previous square from the row below are joined in (80[90:100] rows).

Continuing with col A, pick up and knit 40[45:50] sts down the side of the next square, and rep from *.

There will be 5 of these squares, the last being picked up from the edge of the first square. *See* diagram D for how all this fits together.

## Third row of squares

Turn work to wrong side and work this row from this side. Cast on 40[45:50] sts for first square, and you are now joining on the wrong side rows, to join in with the last square of row 2.

Make the square as usual following the pattern below from * Row 2. To make the pattern as before, reverse the knits and purls because you begin on the wrong side.

For the rest of row 3 squares, pick up and purl 40[45:50] sts down side of previous square using col A.

**\* Row 2** Purl.

**Row 3** S1, K38[43:48], P2 tog (last st + 1st st of next square], turn.

**Row 4** Purl. Change to col B or C.

**Row 5** Purl [purling the last 2 together to join as before).

**Row 6** Knit.

Rep until 6 squares are made in this row of squares, keeping the stitches at armholes and neck on a stitch holder.

## Fourth row of squares

Turn and follow the directions for second row of squares, making 7 more as in the diagram, keeping stitches on holders for the armholes and neck.

## Fifth row of squares

Another wrong side row, so follow the pattern as in row 3 for third row of squares. This time, pick up and make squares following diagram D to make 4 altogether, leaving gaps for armholes. Put the stitches on holders at the end of each square to use for neckband and sleeve joining.

For sleeves, neck and finishing, follow 'short version' instructions.

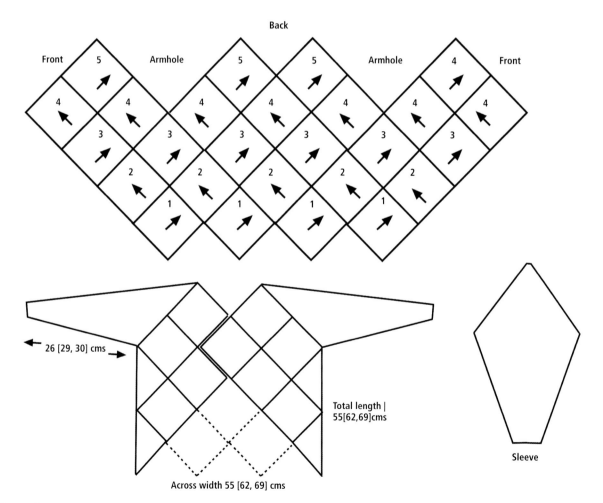

*Pattern 9, diagram D: measurements.*

# Zig-zag rib waistcoat

## Materials

Fine hemp (*see* Further Information).
Natural 200–250g (7–9oz) col B (680–850m), 50g
(1¾oz) col A (170m).

## Needles

Size 3mm (US2:UK11). You also need a double-ended or
circular needle – *see* row 6.

## Size

To fit bust 86[92:98]cm (32[36:38]in).

See note at the end: the waistcoat will be longer after
washing by a few centimetres (inches). To work this out, knit
a sample and measure it. Wash it and measure again. Count
the stripes in the instructions to work out the finished length.

## Tension

28 sts to 10cm (4in) measured over flat stocking stitch, but
over the zigzags it is 28 sts to 8cm (3in).

## Knitting level

Moderate/advanced.

Pattern 10, colour codes.

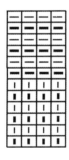

Pattern 10, stitch chart.

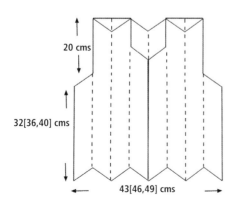

Pattern 10, diagram and measurements.

## Construction

Knitted in one piece with no side seams. The zigzags are formed by increasing and decreasing in pairs at regular intervals, which must be kept in line.

## Body

The pattern is knitted with 16[18:22] sts for each 'zig', and 16[18:22] for each 'zag'.

It may help to keep markers at these points between each pair of increases and decreases, as they must be kept in line. Change from knit side stocking st to purl side stocking st in each stripe of 6 rows.

Using col A, cast on 256[288:352] sts. Leave this thread hanging, and link it up the side of the rows as you go. Change to col B, and begin pattern.

**Row 1** * K2 tog, K13[15:19], knit into front and back of next st (= 16[18:22] sts), knit into front and back of next st, K13[15:19], S1, K1, psso (=16[18: 22] sts) *; rep from * to * to end.

**Row 2** Purl.

**Row 3** As row 1.

**Row 4** As row 2.

**Row 5** As row 1. Leave yarn hanging.

**Row 6** Slide the sts back to where col A thread is hanging, and knit a row using col A. Leave thread again and carry it up the side until next row 6, linking it in.

Turn, so that purl side is facing, and now begin again from row 1 using col B, working the same pattern (to make a knit-faced stripe), except that the shaping in rows 1, 3 and 5 will read: * K2 tog, K12[14:18], knit into front and back of next st,

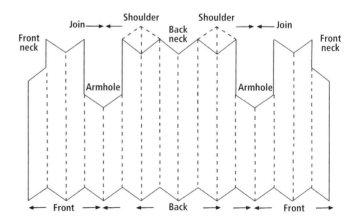

Increases and decreases

knit into front and back of next st, K14[16:20], S1, K1, psso *; rep from * to * to end. This is to keep the incs and decs in line. Work 6 rows.

Continue in this way working 5 rows col B, 1 row col A, with the knit and purl sides alternating in each stripe, until there are 15[17:19] lots of 6-row stripes complete (90[102:114] rows).

**NB:** this will look short at present. The measurements on the diagram show the approximate finished length, which changes after washing: see note at the end of this pattern.

## Divide for armholes

Keeping the pattern the same, leave 64[72:88] sts for each front on holders, and work on 128[144:176] sts for back. Cast off 16[18:22] sts at armhole edge on beg of next 2 rows, leaving the centre 96[108:132] sts. Work straight in the same pattern until there are 12 lots of 6-row stripes from armhole, and leave sts on spare thread.

## Shoulder

*Back:* Working on the shoulder zigzag (32[36:44] sts) and leaving the centre zigzag for the neck on a stitch holder, cont in pattern, decreasing in centre, with no increases at the edges, and also making an extra decrease on row 6 of pattern. The fabric will now get rapidly smaller (*see diagram*); work until all sts have gone, pulling thread through to fasten off.

*Fronts:* Cast off 16[18:22] sts for armhole, and work straight in pattern on the remaining 48[54:66] sts until there are 5 lots of 6-row stripes from the armholes.

## Neck

Cast off the 16[18:22] sts at neck edge, and continue on the remaining 32[36:44] sts until it measures the same as the back.

## Joining the shoulder

This piece will now fit into the shaped back shoulder zigzag. Using a needle and thread, join as described in Chapter 6, grafting the stitches from the front shoulder and sewing to the back.

## Front bands

Using col B, with right side facing pick up and knit 4 sts to every stripe along the front edges. Work in stocking stitch with purl as right side. Work for 2cm (¾in) and cast off loosely.

## Neck and armholes

Crochet a contrast edge using col A around the neck and armholes to give a finished edge.

## Finishing

Natural hemp yarn needs washing to soften it, and it also drops, becoming longer after washing.

Wash the waistcoat by hand, using a gentle detergent, and a fabric softener in the final rinse. Spin dry and dry flat if possible, then iron. This gives it the characteristic sheen and attractive drape.

---

**Suggestions**

This design can be knitted in wool or other materials to produce a completely different garment.

Wool is springier than hemp, and the knit and purl stripes will want to close up in a ribbed effect, making a very warm fabric: *see photos and Chapter 5.* These instructions could be followed in wool, allowing for extra length, to make a more closely fitted waistcoat.

*Pattern 10, the same design knitted in wool.*

# Baby's waistcoat

## Materials

DK cotton, 200–300g (7–10½oz) col A (520–780m), with small amounts of cols B, C and D.
The illustration is knitted in Paton's Eco Cotton.

## Needles

Size 4mm (US6:UK8) straight or circular

## Size

To fit chest 56[60:64]cm (22¼[23½:25]in).
There are 8 squares round this waistcoat, 4 across the front and 4 across the back. Each square needs to measure 7[7.5:8]cm (2¾[3:3¼]in).

## Tension

The 31-st square measures 7cm (2¾in). To alter sizing, *see* beginning of Chapter 7.

## Knitting level

Easy. Modular knitting with picked-up edges.

## Construction

This waistcoat is made up from modular squares. The squares are knitted in garter stitch with a stocking stitch stripe, then changing colour half way through, sometimes with stripes. *See* the main photograph opposite for order of knitting the squares, and where to place the colours.

## Square 1

Using col A, cast on 31[33:35] sts.
**\* Row 2** Knit.
**Row 3** K14[15:16], S1, knit 2 tog, psso, K14[15:16].
**Row 4** Knit.
**Row 5** Change to col C, K13[14:15], dec as before, purl 13[14:15].
**Row 6** Using col C, purl.
**Row 7** Change back to col A, K12[13:14], dec as before, K12[13:14].
Cont in this way in garter st, decreasing in the centre of every right-side row, until there are 17[19:21] sts left.
Change colour (*see* picture for colours and pattern), and continue in garter st for the rest of the square, finishing when there are 3 sts left.
Next row) S1, K2 tog, psso, and pull thread through. \*

## Square 2

Using col A, cast on 15[16:17] sts, then with right side facing, pick up 16[17:18] sts along the side of Square 1: *see* diagram. Follow instructions for Square 1 from \* to \*.

## Square 3

Using col A, pick up 15[16:17] sts along side of Square 1, 1 at the corner, and 15[16:17] sts along side of Square 1: see diagram. Work the same as Square 1.
Now follow the diagram, and where the squares are between others, pick up all the sts from the previous edges. Otherwise, cast on edges where needed.

## Body

Build up the shape for the back and fronts in one piece as in the diagram, leaving armhole as indicated.
Adjust to the length you want, making either more squares below the armhole, or picking up sts from the bottom edge and adding stripes (as in main photo), picking up 15[16:17] sts per square, and knitting downwards for the required length.

*Pattern 11, colour codes.*

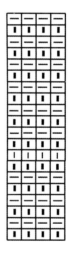

*Pattern 11, stitch chart.*

## Front neck shaping

*See* diagram for position of front neck squares.
Work a triangle or half-square for front of neck by picking up 15[16:17] sts from side of one previous square, working in the usual pattern, and decreasing 1 st at neck edge corner on alt rows in place of the usual central decrease.

## Neck and front bands

Choose a colour and pick up sts along fronts and round neck on one circular needle, picking up 15[16:17] sts per square. Knit in garter stitch, knitting back and forth, for 6 rows, in 2-row stripes of different colours, or plain colour. Make buttonholes if needed (follow the instructions in Chapter 6), or make crochet loops later. Cast off, being careful to keep it looser round the bend where the neck joins the front bands.

## Armhole bands

Pick up 15[16:17] sts per square from base of armhole over shoulder and down the other side, but not across the underarm edge, and work in garter st back and forth, but in 'short rows' (the illustration shows 2-row stripes) as follows:
Knit the first 2 rows,
**Row 3** Knit to last 6 sts, turn.
**Row 4** Knit to last 6 sts, turn.
**Row 5** Knit to last 12 sts, turn.
**Row 6** Knit to last 12 sts, turn.
Continue in this way, leaving 6 more sts behind and turning the knitting so the armband becomes wider at the top of the shoulder. When you are working on only 12[14:16] sts, knit to the end of the row again, and cast off the whole armband.

## Finishing

Finish underarm edge with a row of single crochet, sew in ends and attach buttons.

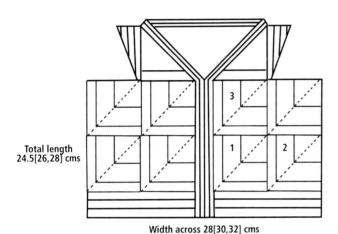

Total length 24.5[26,28] cms

Width across 28[30,32] cms

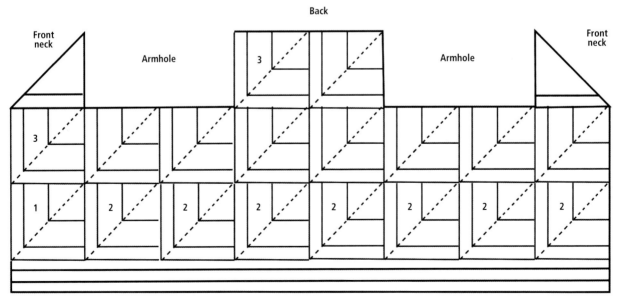

*Pattern 11, diagram and measurements.*

# Child's modular jumper

## Materials

DK cotton. The illustration is knitted in a mixture of cottons including Wendy Supreme with pattern in the dyed yarn, and Rowan Milk Cotton.

Total weight of yarn: 350[375:400]g (12¼[13¼:14]oz )

Main cols B and D 150g (5½oz) each (360m), 50g (1¾oz) col A (120m), 50g (1¾oz) col C (120m).

## Needles

Size 4mm (US6:UK8) straight or circular (a circular needle is useful for the top of the sleeve).

## Size

There are 10 squares around this jumper.

To fit chest 65[70:75]cm (25½[27½:29½]in): see diagram B for actual size. Each square needs to measure 7[7.5:8]cm (2¾[3:3¼]in.

## Knitting level

Easy.

*Pattern 12, colour codes.*

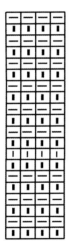

*Pattern 12, stitch chart.*

## Construction

This jumper is made up from squares that are linked as they are knitted. The squares are cast on (or picked up from previous squares) along 2 sides, and decreased in the centre of alternate rows to form the square shape, with the rows turning a right angle.

The squares are knitted in garter stitch, with a stocking stitch stripe, then changing colour half way through. *See* diagram A and main photo for order of knitting the squares, and where to place the colours.

## Square 1

*See* main photo for order of colours. Each square cahn be different, so below is a guide to where the colours change.
Using col B or D, cast on 29[31:33] sts.
**Row 2** * Knit.
**Row 3** K13[14:15], S1, K2 tog, psso, K13[14:15].
**Row 4** Knit.
**Row 5** Change col, K12[13:14], dec as before, P12[13:14].
**Row 6** Purl.
**Row 7** Change col again, K11[12:13], dec as before, K11[12:13].
Cont in this way in garter st, decreasing in the centre of every right-side row, until there are 15[17:19] sts left.

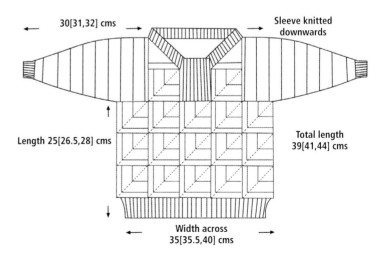

*Pattern 12, diagram B: measurements.*

Change col for the final corner, and continue in garter st for the rest of the square, finishing when there are 3 sts left. Next row) S1, K2 tog, psso, and pull thread through. *

## Square 2

Using col A, cast on 14[15:16] sts then with right side facing, pick up 15[16:17] sts along the side of Square 1: *see* diagram A. You should pick up sts from the cast-on loops on Square 1. Follow instructions from * to *.

## Square 3

Using col A, with right side facing, pick up 15[16:17] sts along the side of Square 1, then cast on 14[15:16] sts. *See* diagram A, and work the same as Square 1.
Now follow the diagram, and where the squares are between others, pick up all the sts from the previous edges. Otherwise, cast on edges where needed.
Build up the shape for the back, then continue round the side to the front as in the diagram, leaving armhole as indicated, and shaping only for front neck.

## Front neck shaping

*See* diagram A for position of front neck squares.
Work a triangle or half-square either side of front of neck by picking up 14[15:16] sts from side of one previous square, working in the usual pattern, and decreasing 1 st at neck edge corner on alt rows in place of the usual central decrease.

## Sleeves

Sleeves are worked from the top down. Join the shoulders (*see* Chapter 6).
With right side of garment facing and col B, pick up the stitches from the bottom of the armhole to the shoulder, then down to armhole, but not across the underarm edge. Pick up and knit 14[15:16] sts per square (56[60:64] sts over the 4 squares).

*Pattern:* * Work in garter st using col B for 10 rows, then change to col A.
Work 2 rows stocking st, then repeat from *, in stripes of 10 rows col B or D, 2 rows col A or C. When sleeve measures

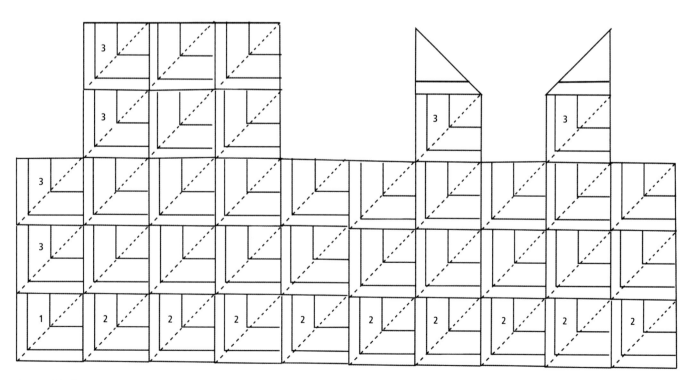

*Pattern 12, diagram A: construction.*

6.5[7:7.5]cm (2½[2¾:3]in), decrease 1 st at each end of next and every following 12th row.
Continue until sleeve measures 27[28:29]cm (10½[11:11½]in) or the length you want.

*Cuff:* Work in K2, P2 rib in 2-row stripes of A and B for 3cm (1¼in), and cast off loosely.

## Bottom welt

The bottom edge can be left as the final edge, or a welt added to adjust the length.
Using col B, pick up and knit 15[16:17] sts from each square along the bottom edge. You can knit the welt in the round, or make a separate back and front, leaving a slit at the side.
Knit back 1 row using col B, then work in K2, P2 rib in 2-row stripes of A and B until it is the length you want, and cast off.

## Neck

*Front placket:* Using col B, pick up 20[22:24] sts along the bottom edge of the front opening, and work in 2-row stripes of A and B in K2, P2 rib until it is as long as the neighbouring square. Put the stitches onto a stitch holder, and knit another piece, again picking up from the bottom edge behind the first piece, putting stitches onto a holder when it is the same length as the first piece.

*Neckband:* Using col B and starting at front of right placket, work in ribbing, then pick up and knit 18[19:20]sts from the front diagonal square, 14[15:16] sts from each square along back of neck, and 18[19:20]sts along left front diagonal.
Work in K2, P2 rib across the second front placket, then continue in K2, P2 rib in 2-row stripes of A and B for 3cm (1¼in) or as long as required, in stripes or plain colour. Cast off.

## Finishing

Sew down the right-side edge of the underneath placket, and the left-side edge of the top placket, so they are overlapping but both open at the central edge.
Make a crochet button loop on the top edge and sew a button to match on the underneath edge.
Sew the side seam and underarm seams.

*Detail of front placket and opening.*

# Baby's smock-dress

## Materials

DK cotton, 25g (1oz) col A (60m), 50[75:80]g (1¾[2¾:3]oz) each of cols B, C and D (120m, 180m, 192m).
The illustration is knitted in Wendy Supreme (with pattern in the dyeing), and Paton's Eco Cotton.

## Needles

Size 3.75mm (US5:UK9): 1 x 60cm (24in) circular needle; 1 x 40cm (16in) circular needle or 4 double-pointed needles for the ribbed yoke.

## Size

Actual measurement across skirt (see diagram): 38[42:44] cm (15[16½:17¼]in). This makes a dress for a 3[6:9]-month-old baby girl, but as she grows it can be worn as a smock-top.

## Tension

25 sts of zigzag pattern to 10cm (4in).

## Knitting level

Moderate.

*Pattern 13, colour codes.*

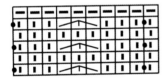

*Pattern 13, stitch chart.*

## Construction

The skirt is knitted in the round, in a zigzag pattern. The bodice is in K2, P2 rib, so will stretch to fit the growing baby.

## Skirt

Using col A, cast on 190[210:220] sts.

Knit one round. Break off yarn, and weave in the end on the next round. Begin pattern using col B.

**Round 1** * Knit into front and back of stitch (to make 2 sts), K3, S1, K2 tog, psso, K2, knit into front and back of next st; * rep from * to * all round.

**Round 2** Knit.

**Round 3** As round 1.

**Round 4** Knit.

**Round 5** Using col C, as round 1.

**Round 6** Using col C, purl.

Repeat these 6 rounds with rounds 1–4 using col D, rounds 5 and 6 using col A, then again with rounds 1–4 using col B, rounds 5 and 6 using col C.

Continue using the colours in this order until skirt measures 18[20:22]cm (7[8:8½]in) finishing on round 6. (Adjust here to the length you want.)

Knit 1 round using col C, then purl 1 round using col C, decreasing 22[26:28] sts evenly, so you have 168[184:192] sts (decrease every 8th or 9th st all round).

Change to col B, knit 1 round.

Now work in K2, P2 rib, beginning with another round in col B, then in 2-row stripes of colours C, D, C, B, repeated.

When the ribbing measures 8[9:10]cm (3[3½:4]in), divide in half for front and back, leaving 84[92:96] sts on a holder, and working on the other 84[92:96] sts.

## Back

Cast off 6[7:8] sts at beg of next 2 rows, then cast off 2 sts at beg of next 4 rows. *

Now decrease1 st each end of every row until there are 48[50:52] sts left.

Work straight until back measures 5[6:7]cm (2[2¼:2¾]in) from the armholes, then cast off the centre 14[16:18] sts, leaving 17 for each shoulder.

Working on one shoulder at a time, cast off 1 st at neck edge every row until there are 6 sts left and work until back measures 10cm (4in) from the armhole. Cast off (or keep on a holder for grafting together with the front).

## Front

Shape the armholes as for the back until *, then begin front neck shaping. Divide in half, and working on one half at a time, continue shaping the armhole edge as for the back, but also decrease at neck edge every row until there are 22 sts, then on alt rows until there are 6 sts and it is the same length as the back.

Cast off, or put the stitches with the 6 sts from the back and sew or graft the shoulders together (*see* Chapter 6).

## Finishing

Using a crochet hook the same size as the knitting needles, work a picot edging in crochet around neck and armholes.

## Picot edge

* Crochet 3 plain sts onto the edge of the knitting, then crochet 2 chain sts (not attached to the knitting). Put the hook back through the last stitch on the knitting and repeat from *.

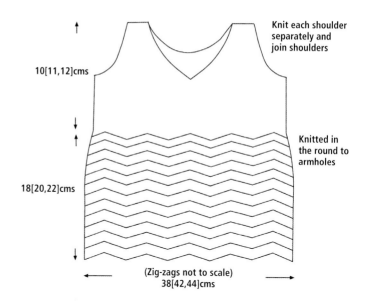

*Pattern 13 diagram and measurements.*

*Detail of picot edge around neck and armholes.*

# GLOSSARY

**basket weave** *see* entrelac.

**bast fibres** fibre obtained from the stems of plants.

**bias** diagonal.

**chemical dyes** manufactured dyes, available in powder form.

**'continental' knitting** knitting with yarn held in left hand.

**darts** *see* flares and gores (all names for shaping by using short rows).

**domino knitting** knitting composed of pieces shaped by increases and decreases that fit together, and are linked by picking up stitches.

**double-cloth knitting** knitting on two needles to produce two separate fabrics joined at the sides.

**entrelac** made by knitting rows of diagonal blocks which link as they go. Also known as basket weave.

**Fair Isle knitting** knitting patterns with two or more colours in each row, stranding or weaving colours on the reverse side. Also known as jacquard knitting.

**flares** *see* darts.

**gores** *see* darts.

**gussets** a shape inserted in a garment where added strength or freedom of movement is needed.

**hank** see also skein. Knitting yarn when reeled in one length into a loose coil, ready for dyeing.

**i-cord** knitted cord of few stitches, made on two needles.

**ikat weaving** patterns in weaving produced by tie-dyeing the yarn before weaving. The shifting of the threads in weaving results in slight blurring of the patterning.

**insets** pieces of knitting set into a shape to make a 3-D effect in modular knitting.

**intarsia** knitting with several colours in a row, each colour keeping to its own area rather than travelling across the row.

**jacquard knitting** *see* Fair Isle.

**k1, s1, psso** also called 'ssk', *see* 'decreases'.

**knitting frame** forerunner of the knitting machine.

**mitred knitting** *see* domino knitting.

**modular knitting** *see* domino knitting.

**mordant** a substance used in preparation for dyeing yarn in 'natural' dyes, which influences the resulting colour and makes it permanent.

**natural dyes** dyes obtained directly from plant or animal material without processing (apart from drying).

**placket** piece of knitting at base of neck opening (*see* project 12).

**short rows** shaping knitting by working incomplete rows so that the shape builds up more on one side than the other. (*See* darts, flares and gores.)

**skein** *see* hank.

**stocking stitch** also called 'stockinette', knit one row, purl one row.

**stranding yarn** carrying the yarn straight across the back of Fair Isle or jacquard knitting.

**weaving in yarn** linking the spare yarn with the yarn being knitted across the back of Fair Isle or jacquard knitting so that it 'weaves' up and down with no loops.

# BIBLIOGRAPHY

## Books on Technique, Stitches and Patterns

Ellen, Alison, *The Handknitter's Design Book*
  (David & Charles, 1992)

Ellen, Alison , *Hand Knitting, New Directions,*
  (Crowood, 2002, paperback 2010)

Fassett, Kaffe, *Glorious Knitting* (Century Publishing, 1985)

*The Harmony Guides to Knitting Stitches* (Lyric Books, 1987)

Norbury, James, *Odham's Encyclopaedia of Knitting*
  (Odham's Press, 1956)

Stanley, Montse, *Knitting, Your Own Designs for a Perfect Fit*
  (David & Charles, 1982)

Stanley, Montse, *The Handknitter's Handbook*
  (David and Charles, 1986)

Stratford, Audrie, *Introducing Knitting* (Batsford, 1972)

Thomas, Mary, *Mary Thomas's Knitting Book*
  (Hodder and Stoughton, 1938)

Thomas, Mary, *Mary Thomas's Book of Knitting Patterns*
  (Hodder and Stoughton, 1943)

Zimmermann, Elizabeth, *Knitting Without Tears*
  (Simon and Schuster, 1971)

## Books on History of Knitting and Traditions

(some including unusual techniques)

Bush, Nancy, *Folk Knitting in Estonia*
  (Interweave Press, 1999)

Collingwood, Peter, *The Maker's Hand: A Close Look
  at Textile Structures* (Bellew Publishing, 1987)

Compton, Rae, *The Complete Book of Traditional Guernsey
  and Jersey Knitting* (Batsford, 1983)

Gainford, Veronica, *Designs for Knitting Kilt Hose and
  Knickerbocker Stockings* (Gainford, 1978)

Gravelle LeCount, Cynthia, *Andean Folk Knitting*
  (Dos Tejedoras Fiber Arts Publications, 1990)

Hinchcliffe, Frances, *Knit One, Purl One: Historic and
  Contemporary Knitting from the V & A's Collection*
  (V&A Museum, 1985)

McGregor, Sheila, *Traditional Fairisle Knitting* (Batsford 1981)

McGregor, Sheila, *Traditional Scandanavian Knitting*
  (Batsford 1983)

Pearson, Michael, *Traditional Knitting* (Collins, 1984)

Rutt, Richard, A History of Handknitting (Batsford, 1987)

Sundbø, Annemore, *Invisible Threads in Knitting*
  (Torridal Tweed, 2007)

Thompson, Gladys, *Guernsey and Jersey Patterns*
  (Batsford, 1969)

Turney, Joanne, *The Culture of Knitting* (Berg, 2009)

## New Wave

Gschwandtner, Sabrina, *Knit Knit: Profiles and Projects from
  Knitting's New Wave* (Stewart, Tabori & Chang, 2007)

# FURTHER INFORMATION

## Suppliers

**Texere Yarns**
College Mill
Barkerend Road, Bradford
West Yorkshire, BD1 4AU
www.texere-yarns.co.uk
*A range of dyed and undyed yarns, natural and man-made, plain and fancy*

**George Weil and Fibrecrafts**
Old Portsmouth Road
Peasmarsh, Guildford
Surrey, GU3 1LZ
www.fibrecrafts.com
*Textile suppliers: materials, dyes, books and publications*

**The House of Hemp**
Beeston Farm
Marhamchurch
Cornwall, EX23 0ET
www.thehouseofhemp.co.uk
*Suppliers of hemp yarn and knitting kits*

**Diamond Fibres**
Diamonds Farm
Horam, East Sussex, TN21 0HF
www.diamondfibres.co.uk
*Commission spinners of worsted knitting yarn*

**Kemtex Educational Supplies**
Chorley Business & Technology Centre
Euxton Lane
Chorley, Lancashire, PR7 6TE
www.kemtex.co.uk
*Suppliers of dyes for wool and other fibres*

## Buttons

Some of the buttons illustrated in this book are made in natural wood, dyed by the author. The basic buttons are available from:

**Chris Baker**
Woodpeckers
Kiln Lane, Lacey Green
Buckinghamshire, HP27 0PT

## Some Organizations Running Courses in Knitting

West Dean College
West Dean
Chichester
West Sussex, PO18 0QZ
www.westdean.org.uk/college

**Missenden Abbey**
Evreham Adult Learning Centre
Swallow Street, Iver
Buckinghamshire, SL0 0HS
www.missendenabbey-al.co.uk

**The Association of Guilds of Weavers, Spinners and Dyers**
www.wsd.org.uk
*With regional branches in each county in the UK, regular meetings are held, and lectures and workshops include hand knitting.*

**The Knitting and Crochet Guild of Great Britain**
www.knitting-and-crochet-guild.org.uk
*Regional branches hold meetings, lectures and workshops.*

# INDEX